Cryptocurrency

BASICS

A Beginner's Guide to Understanding Digital Currencies

Eliza Finley

TABLE OF CONTENTS

INTRODUCTION

Welcome to "Cryptocurrency Basics: A Beginner's Guide to Understanding Digital Currencies." Cryptocurrencies have become an innovative idea in this era of technology, revolutionizing how we see and use money. You've come to the right place if you're interested in this fascinating and constantly changing world of digital currencies but feel overpowered by the terminology and complexity involved.

This e-book is intended to serve as a thorough and user-friendly introduction to cryptocurrency. It will provide you with a solid foundation to effectively navigate the intriguing world of cryptocurrencies, whether you're a curious person eager to learn more or an aspirant investor looking to enter this profitable industry.

The mysteries behind this revolutionary notion will be revealed in the first chapter, "Understanding Cryptocurrency?" We'll look at the underlying ideas behind digital currencies and how they vary from conventional fiat currency. Before delving into the more complex facets of the crypto realm, it is essential to understand the foundations.

We must explore blockchain, the revolutionary technology underpinning cryptocurrencies, to understand its core. The second chapter, "Understanding Blockchain Technology," will detail the decentralized, immutable ledger that forms the basis of every cryptocurrency. You'll have a comprehensive understanding of how blockchain technology operates by the end of this chapter, as well as the potential applications it has outside of banking.

The history of Bitcoin, the first and most famous cryptocurrency, will next be discussed. We will learn about the enigmatic founder, the processes involved in creating Bitcoin, and its significance in influencing the cryptocurrency industry in the chapter "The Birth of Bitcoin."

But Bitcoin isn't the only thing in the crypto realm. We'll introduce you to several notable digital currencies in "Exploring Other Major Cryptocurrencies," each with distinctive features and use cases. This chapter will give you insights into the wide range of cryptocurrencies and assist you in appreciating each one's unique advantages.

Eventually, as you learn more about cryptocurrencies, you'll want to know how to purchase and keep these digital assets safely. In Chapter 5, "How to Buy and Store Cryptocurrencies," you'll learn how to pick a trustworthy exchange, set up a secure wallet, and protect your valuable assets.

In chapter six, we'll detail cryptocurrency mining, a critical component of the crypto world. You'll learn about the function of mining, various consensus methods, and environmental issues connected to this resource-intensive procedure.

In chapter seven, "The Mechanics of Cryptocurrency Transactions," we'll examine how transactions occur within the cryptocurrency network. You'll learn more about the inner workings of cryptographic transactions, including public and private keys, the functions of miners and nodes, and more.

Anyone interested in investing in or using cryptocurrencies must understand their economics. The supply and demand dynamics, the variables impacting cryptocurrency values, and the market's intrinsic volatility will all be covered in Chapter 8, "The Economics of Cryptocurrencies," of the e-book.

The crypto environment has difficulties, though. In chapter nine, "Legal and Regulatory Landscape," we'll look at how government laws are constantly changing, how they may affect taxes, and how crucial compliance is in this area.

In the subsequent chapters, we'll discuss Initial Coin Offerings (ICOs), security issues, and probable future developments in the cryptocurrency field.

Therefore, "Cryptocurrency Basics: A Beginner's Guide to Understanding Digital Currencies" will give you the information and confidence necessary to navigate the exciting world of cryptocurrencies, whether you're an experienced investor trying to diversify your portfolio or a beginner with an insatiable curiosity about it. Together, let's go on this fascinating journey to discover the potential and mysteries of cryptocurrencies.

CHAPTER I

Understanding Cryptocurrency

What is Cryptocurrency?

In the digital age, cryptocurrencies have emerged as a disruptive force in the financial world. Cryptocurrencies, which were created in response to the need for decentralized and secure financial systems, have triggered a revolution that disrupts established ideas about money and banking. In this section, we will explore the concept of cryptocurrency, its underlying principles, and its significance in the modern economy. Understanding cryptocurrencies and how they work is essential for anyone navigating this fascinating and rapidly evolving landscape.

Cryptocurrency, a portmanteau of "crypto" and "currency," was introduced to the world with the launch of Bitcoin in 2009. A whitepaper proposing a peer-to-peer electronic cash system based on a decentralized ledger referred to as the blockchain was published by an unidentified entity using the pseudonym Satoshi Nakamoto. This groundbreaking paper laid the foundation for a new era of digital currencies.

Cryptocurrency is fundamentally a digital or virtual currency that uses cryptographic methods to ensure the security of financial transactions, govern the creation of new units, and authenticate the transfer of assets. Unlike traditional fiat currencies issued and regulated by central authorities, cryptocurrencies operate on decentralized networks, providing a degree of autonomy and transparency that sets them apart.

Cryptocurrencies function through a distributed and immutable ledger known as the blockchain. This ledger keeps track of every transaction made over a computer network, ensuring that no single entity has full authority over the system. Transactions are grouped into "blocks" and linked to the previous block, creating an unbroken information chain. This decentralized nature ensures that cryptocurrencies resist censorship and fraud, as there is no central point of failure.

One of the fundamental aspects of cryptocurrencies is their decentralized nature. They operate without a central authority or intermediary, enabling peer-to-peer transactions and disintermediation of financial systems. This characteristic empowers individuals to have direct control over their funds and removes the need to rely on traditional banking institutions.

Cryptocurrencies employ advanced cryptographic algorithms to secure transactions and protect users from fraud and hacking attempts. The cryptographic nature of cryptocurrencies ensures the integrity and privacy of financial transactions, making them highly secure and tamper-resistant.

Depending on the cryptocurrency, users can enjoy varying levels of anonymity and privacy in their transactions. While Bitcoin transactions are pseudonymous, meaning they are associated with addresses rather than personal identities, other cryptocurrencies like Monero offer enhanced privacy features that make transactions untraceable.

Many cryptocurrencies have a fixed supply or predetermined issuance schedule, reducing inflation risk and ensuring scarcity akin to precious metals like gold. For instance, Bitcoin has a capped supply of 21 million coins, making it a deflationary asset.

Cryptocurrencies transcend borders, allowing users worldwide to participate in the global financial ecosystem without the need for traditional banking infrastructure. As long as users have access to the internet, they can send and receive cryptocurrencies worldwide in a matter of minutes, facilitating cross-border transactions with ease.

Beyond Bitcoin, the cryptocurrency market boasts diverse digital assets with unique features and use cases. When Ethereum was released in 2015, it established the idea of "smart contracts," which enabled the development of decentralized apps (DApps) on its blockchain. Ripple (XRP) aims to revolutionize cross-border payments by facilitating faster and cheaper transactions. Litecoin, often called "digital silver," was created as a lighter and more accessible version of Bitcoin, with faster transaction confirmation times.

Mining is an essential process in cryptocurrency, particularly in networks that utilize Proof-of-Work (PoW) consensus mechanisms. Miners validate and record transactions by solving complex mathematical puzzles, adding them to the blockchain in exchange for rewards. This process secures the network and regulates the creation of new coins, maintaining the system's integrity and preventing double-spending.

Cryptocurrencies are not without challenges and risks. Price volatility remains a prominent concern, with prices subject to fluctuations influenced by market sentiment, regulatory developments, and technological advancements. The speculative nature of the market can lead to significant price swings, making cryptocurrencies a high-risk investment for some.

Security breaches, hacking incidents, and scams threaten users' and cryptocurrencies' overall credibility. Though blockchain technology is secure, vulnerabilities in exchanges, wallets, and smart contracts can lead to significant losses if malicious actors exploit it.

Moreover, the cryptocurrencies regulatory landscape is still evolving, with various countries implementing different approaches to cryptocurrency taxation, legal recognition, and regulatory oversight. These uncertainties create challenges for businesses and investors seeking to navigate the legal aspects of the crypto world.

The future of cryptocurrencies is a topic of immense speculation. Advocates believe cryptocurrencies will revolutionize finance and empower individuals by offering greater financial freedom and inclusivity. Blockchain-based decentralized finance (DeFi) applications have already demonstrated the potential to disrupt established financial services like lending, borrowing, even decentralized exchanges.

On the other hand, skeptics raise concerns about regulatory hurdles, technological limitations, and potential risks associated with the rapid expansion of this nascent market. Although it's important for market stability and consumer safety, regulatory oversight can also inhibit innovation and prevent the widespread adoption of cryptocurrencies.

Cryptocurrencies have emerged as a transformative force, challenging conventional financial systems and reshaping how we perceive money. As decentralized and secure digital assets, cryptocurrencies offer exciting possibilities for the future of finance. However, understanding the nuances of this complex ecosystem is essential for anyone seeking to participate in this fascinating world. With ongoing advancements and growing acceptance, cryptocurrencies are poised to leave a lasting impact on the global economy, marking a new chapter in the history of money and finance. As we continue to explore the potential and risks of cryptocurrencies, it is crucial to approach this revolutionary technology with caution, understanding, and an open mind. Only then can we fully appreciate the transformative power and opportunities that cryptocurrencies offer to individuals and societies worldwide.

The Evolution of Money

The development of human civilization has been significantly influenced by the use of money as a medium of exchange. The idea of money has continuously changed to match the shifting demands of society, from prehistoric trading systems to the sophisticated financial instruments of the modern period. In this section, we will explore the fascinating journey of money, tracing its origins from ancient times to the digital age. Understanding the evolution of money provides valuable insights into the development of economies and the significant impact money has on human interactions and progress.

The earliest form of trade involved the direct exchange of goods and services without any standardized medium of exchange. Known as bartering, this system prevailed in ancient societies where people traded commodities they had a surplus in exchange for goods or services they required. While bartering facilitated basic transactions, it had inherent limitations, such as the need for a double coincidence of wants and the impracticality of dividing certain goods.

To overcome the challenges of bartering, societies began using commodities with inherent value as a medium of exchange. Items such as cowrie shells, salt, and precious metals like gold and silver served as commodity money. These items were easily recognizable, durable, and divisible, making them ideal for facilitating trade. Commodity money marked a significant step towards standardized value representation in economic transactions.

As economies expanded, the demand for a more reliable and standardized medium of exchange grew. This led to the establishment of metallic standards, where coins made from precious metals were minted with designated denominations. The value of these coins was determined by the weight and purity of the metal they contained, providing greater consistency and trust in transactions.

Carrying precious metal coins for large transactions became impractical, leading to the adoption of paper money as a representation of value backed by a reserve of precious metals. In the 17th century, banks began issuing paper notes, and governments eventually took over issuing currency. This marked the transition to fiat money, where the currency's value was based on trust and confidence in the issuing authority rather than its intrinsic value.

In the 19th and early 20th centuries, the gold standard gained prominence, where the value of a country's currency was pegged to a specific amount of gold. This system provided stability and limited the ability of governments to print excessive amounts of money. However, the rigidity of the gold standard also constrained economic flexibility during times of crisis. During the 20th century, the majority of nations abandoned the gold standard, which sparked the growth of fiat currencies that had no connection to precious metals.

Advancements in technology, particularly the rise of the internet, paved the way for the development of digital money. Electronic payments, credit cards, and online banking transformed how individuals conduct financial transactions. This digital revolution made transactions more convenient and laid the groundwork for the emergence of cryptocurrencies.

In 2009, Bitcoin, the first decentralized cryptocurrency, was introduced worldwide. Bitcoin's creation, based on blockchain technology, marked a radical departure from traditional monetary systems. As a digital and decentralized currency, Bitcoin operates outside the control of any central authority, providing individuals with unprecedented financial autonomy and privacy.

Following the success of Bitcoin, a multitude of other cryptocurrencies emerged, each with its unique features and use cases. Ethereum, launched in 2015, introduced smart contracts, enabling the creation of decentralized applications and the concept of programmable money. Ripple (XRP) aimed to revolutionize cross-border payments, and other cryptocurrencies offered specialized solutions for various industries.

As digital currencies gained traction, central banks worldwide began exploring the concept of Central Bank Digital Currencies (CBDCs). CBDCs, which combine the advantages of digital currencies with the security and support of conventional fiat currencies, would be issued and governed by central banks. CBDCs have the power to change the way the world's financial system operates and promote financial inclusion.

As the evolution of money continues, it raises questions about the future of financial transactions. Cryptocurrencies and digital currencies challenge traditional banking systems, offering new opportunities for financial services and global trade. A paradigm shift in finance is being signaled by the increasing utilization of blockchain technology and the possibility of more effective, transparent, and secure transactions.

Why Cryptocurrencies Matter

Cryptocurrencies have emerged as a transformative force, capturing the world's attention and challenging traditional financial systems. Cryptocurrencies have changed how we think about money, finance, and trust. They were created out of a need for decentralized and secure financial transactions. This section will explore why cryptocurrencies matter and their significance in the modern world. From their potential to democratize financial access to their impact on global economies, understanding why cryptocurrencies matter is essential to grasping their implications for individuals, businesses, and societies.

Cryptocurrencies' potential to advance financial inclusion and empowerment is one of the most compelling reasons they matter. Traditional banking systems often exclude large portions of the global population, particularly in developing countries with limited access to banking services. Cryptocurrencies provide a different type of financial environment that anybody with a connection to the internet can access, enabling anyone, regardless of socioeconomic background, to take charge of their finances and engage in the global economy.

Cryptocurrencies do not rely on the physical infrastructure of banks, allowing individuals in remote or underbanked regions to transact and store value securely. For the unbanked population, historically excluded from financial services, cryptocurrencies provide a gateway to participate in the global economy, send and receive remittances, and access financial tools that were once out of reach.

Cryptocurrencies operate on decentralized networks, eliminating the need for intermediaries like banks to facilitate transactions. Decentralization fosters trustless transactions, where parties can engage in peer-to-peer exchanges without relying on a central authority. This reduces transaction costs and mitigates the risk of censorship, fraud, and government interference, making cryptocurrencies appealing for those seeking greater financial autonomy.

Removing intermediaries from the financial system enables quicker and more efficient transactions, as there are no delays associated with traditional banking processes. Users have direct control over their funds, reducing the risk of frozen funds or transactions being blocked by third parties. This decentralized nature is particularly crucial in regions with political instability or where trust in traditional financial institutions is low.

The high costs and delays associated with traditional remittances and cross-border transactions have long hindered international trade and financial cooperation. Cryptocurrencies enable near-instantaneous and low-cost cross-border transactions, facilitating a more efficient global payment system. Cryptocurrencies offer a potential solution to the challenges posed by traditional international money transfers by eliminating the need for intermediaries and the hassle of foreign exchange regulations.

Remittance flows, which are critical for supporting families in developing countries, can be expedited and made more cost-effective with cryptocurrencies. Migrants can send money back home without paying exorbitant fees, ensuring more funds reach their intended recipients. Moreover, cross-border transactions involving cryptocurrencies are not constrained by the same banking hours and international restrictions, allowing for continuous and unrestricted global trade.

Financial transactions should always be private, and cryptocurrencies provide varied anonymity and privacy. While Bitcoin transactions are pseudonymous, some privacy-focused cryptocurrencies like Monero and Zcash offer enhanced privacy features, making them appealing to individuals who prioritize confidentiality in their financial dealings.

The cryptographic nature of cryptocurrencies provides robust security against fraud and counterfeiting, enhancing the overall safety of financial transactions. Each transaction on the blockchain is immutable, meaning it cannot be altered or tampered with once recorded. This feature makes a higher sense of accountability possible by making sure that every transaction is publicly accessible on the public ledger and lowers the potential of financial crimes such as money laundering.

Blockchain technology, a decentralized, unchangeable record with many real-world uses outside of banking, is at the core of cryptocurrencies. Blockchain's potential extends to supply chain management, voting systems, intellectual property protection, etc. As blockchain technology continues to advance, its adoption across various industries has the potential to revolutionize how we manage data, establish trust, and conduct business transactions.

The transparency and integrity of blockchain technology have the potential to enhance various industries' efficiency, reducing paperwork, eliminating fraud, and enabling real-time tracking of goods and services. Furthermore, blockchain-based systems can give consumers more control over their data by letting them decide what information to share and with whom, which lowers the possibility of data breaches as well as unwanted access.

Cryptocurrencies have created a new asset class, presenting unique investment opportunities for individuals and institutional investors. While the crypto market's volatility carries risks, it also offers the potential for substantial returns. Moreover, the rise of cryptocurrencies has spurred financial innovation with the development of decentralized finance (DeFi) platforms, non-fungible tokens (NFTs), and other innovative financial products that challenge traditional financial institutions and services.

DeFi offers a decentralized substitute for conventional financial services, including lending, borrowing, and yield farming by utilizing smart contracts on blockchain platforms. Due to the democratization of financial products, anyone with a web connection can now access various financial services without the assistance of banks or other intermediaries.

The increasing adoption of cryptocurrencies has raised discussions about the impact on national economies and the role of central banks. Some countries have explored the concept of Central Bank Digital Currencies (CBDCs) as a means to leverage blockchain technology while maintaining central bank control over the currency. CBDCs could improve monetary policy, financial stability, and payment efficiency, but they also raise concerns about privacy, financial surveillance, and the role of private cryptocurrencies in the financial ecosystem.

CBDCs could offer benefits such as reducing transaction costs, enabling real-time settlement, and increasing financial inclusion. However, introducing CBDCs also requires careful consideration of regulatory frameworks, cybersecurity measures, and potential effects on monetary policy. The coexistence of private cryptocurrencies and CBDCs presents a complex landscape that requires collaboration between governments, central banks, and the private sector.

While cryptocurrencies offer promising opportunities, they have challenges and regulatory considerations. Price volatility, cybersecurity threats, and potential use in illicit activities have raised concerns among regulators and governments worldwide. As regulators navigate the changing cryptocurrency world, it has become more challenging to balance encouraging innovation and protecting consumers.

Ensuring investor protection, combating money laundering and fraud, and addressing potential market manipulation are pressing issues that regulators and policymakers must address. Additionally, the global nature of cryptocurrencies raises challenges in establishing uniform regulatory frameworks that accommodate the diverse needs and goals of different countries.

CHAPTER II

Understanding Blockchain Technology

What is Blockchain?

Blockchain, a revolutionary technology, has captured the world's attention in recent years, promising to transform various industries and redefine how we exchange and store information. Born as the underlying technology powering the first cryptocurrency, Bitcoin, blockchain has evolved into much more than just a ledger for financial transactions. Blockchain is a distributed, unchangeable digital ledger that keeps track of all transactions between network nodes or computers. An unbroken chain of information is produced by grouping every transaction into a "block" and connecting it to the one before it. Data recorded on the blockchain cannot be changed or withdrawn due to this unique design, providing unprecedented security and transparency.

Blockchain relies on a consensus mechanism in which network members, often called nodes, agree on the legitimacy of transactions before their addition to the blockchain. The most commonly used consensus mechanisms are Proof-of-Work (PoW) and Proof-of-

Stake (PoS). PoW relies on complex computational puzzles that miners must solve to validate transactions and add blocks to the chain. On the other hand, PoS demands that users stake a set amount of their cryptocurrency as collateral in order to approve transactions and add new blocks.

Key characteristics of blockchain include decentralization, immutability, transparency, and security. Decentralization enhances the security and resilience of the system, as there is no single point of failure vulnerable to attacks or manipulation. Once data is recorded on the blockchain, it becomes nearly impossible to alter or delete. Each block contains a unique cryptographic hash, linking it to the previous block, making any tampering evident and preventing data manipulation. All transactions on the blockchain are transparently visible to all network participants, promoting accountability and trust, as users can independently verify the authenticity of transactions and track the flow of information. The cryptographic nature of blockchain ensures that data remains secure from unauthorized access and tampering. Additionally, the decentralized nature of the network reduces the risk of cyberattacks targeting a single point of control.

The birth of blockchain technology emerged in 2009 with the creation of Bitcoin by an anonymous entity known as Satoshi Nakamoto. Bitcoin's blockchain was designed to serve as a secure, decentralized ledger for recording and verifying financial transactions without a central authority. Bitcoin's success paved the way for exploring blockchain technology's potential in various other sectors.

While cryptocurrencies were the initial use case for blockchain technology, their potential extends far beyond digital currencies. Various industries have started exploring blockchain applications to improve efficiency, transparency, and security in their processes. In supply chain management, blockchain can revolutionize the system by providing a transparent and traceable record of the movement of goods, enabling real-time tracking, reducing fraud, and ensuring the authenticity and quality of products. In healthcare, blockchain can improve data management by providing a secure and interoperable platform for storing and sharing medical records, allowing patients to have more control over their data and granting access to healthcare providers as needed.

By reducing voter fraud and guaranteeing the accuracy of results, blockchain-based voting systems can improve the transparency and integrity of elections. Each vote is recorded as an immutable transaction on the blockchain, reducing the risk of manipulation. Blockchain can streamline management in intellectual property by recording ownership, rights, and licensing information on an immutable ledger, reducing disputes and enhancing copyright protection. Smart contracts, self-executing agreements with terms directly written into code, can automate various processes, eliminating the need for intermediaries and ensuring transparent and tamper-resistant execution.

Blockchain technology has enormous potential, but it also has challenges that need to be fixed if it is to become more widely used. One of the primary concerns is scalability. As more transactions are added to the blockchain, the network's capacity to handle them may become limited, leading to slower transaction times and increased fees. Interoperability between blockchains is also challenging, as various blockchain networks often operate independently. Efforts are underway to develop protocols enabling seamless communication and data transfer between blockchain platforms.

Concerns have been expressed about sustainability along with the carbon footprint of cryptocurrencies due to the negative environmental effects of Proof-of-Work (PoW) consensus mechanisms, which are frequently utilized in cryptocurrencies like Bitcoin. To address these concerns, some projects explore alternative consensus mechanisms like Proof-of-Stake (PoS), which consume significantly less energy.

The regulatory landscape surrounding blockchain and cryptocurrencies is evolving, with different countries adopting varying approaches. Regulatory frameworks aim to balance fostering innovation and protecting consumers, investors, and businesses. Establishing clear and coherent regulations is essential to provide legal certainty and encourage responsible growth in blockchain.

In conclusion, blockchain technology has appeared as a transformative force with the potential to revolutionize various industries and reshape how we manage and secure data. Its decentralized, transparent, and safe nature presents unique opportunities for financial inclusion, supply chain management, and data governance. While challenges exist in terms of scalability, environmental impact, and regulatory considerations, the potential benefits of blockchain outweigh these obstacles. By harnessing the power of blockchain responsibly, we can unlock its transformative potential and create a more efficient, transparent, and secure future for various industries and global communities.

How Blockchain Works

One of the most revolutionary technological advancements of the digital age is blockchain technology, the foundation of cryptocurrencies like Bitcoin. Blockchain, at its core, is a decentralized, immutable ledger that records each transaction created among a network of computers. With the ability to offer unprecedented transparency, security, and trust in digital interactions, blockchain has garnered significant attention from various industries. In this section, we will delve into the workings of blockchain, exploring its fundamental components, consensus mechanisms, and the process of adding new transactions to the chain. Understanding how blockchain works is crucial for unlocking its potential across finance, supply chain management, healthcare, and numerous other sectors.

At the heart of blockchain technology lies its decentralized nature, which sets it apart from traditional centralized systems. In a centralized system, a single authority (e.g., a central bank or a company) controls data and transactions. The blockchain, in contrast, runs on a distributed network of computers called nodes, each of which has a copy of the entire ledger. This decentralized structure eliminates the need for a central authority, increasing the network's resilience and removing the risk of a single point of failure.

By guaranteeing that no single party can modify or alter the data on the blockchain, decentralization fosters user trust and transparency. When a new transaction is recorded on the blockchain, it undergoes a verification process, and a consensus must be reached among the nodes to add the transaction to the chain. This consensus mechanism ensures that all nodes agree on the transaction's validity, preventing fraudulent or malicious activities.

In a blockchain, transactions are grouped in blocks. Each block contains a list of valid transactions, a timestamp, and a unique cryptographic hash identifier. The hash is a mathematical function that converts the block's data into a fixed-size string of characters. This hash acts as a digital fingerprint for the block, ensuring that any change to the data in the block would result in a different hash. Each block's hash also includes the previous block's hash, creating a chain of linked blocks.

The link between blocks through their hashes creates an unbroken sequence, making it nearly impossible to tamper with past transactions. Altering data in one block would change its hash, leading to a mismatch with the next block's hash and the subsequent blocks in the chain. As a result, the integrity of the entire chain would be compromised, and the tampering attempt would be evident.

Mining is a crucial process in blockchain networks that employs consensus mechanisms to agree on the validity of transactions and add new blocks to the chain. The most well-known consensus mechanisms are Proof-of-Work (PoW) and Proof-of-Stake (PoS).

In Proof of Work, miners compete to figure out difficult mathematical puzzles tied to each block. The first miner to finish the puzzle publishes the answer to the network, demonstrating their use of computer resources. Other nodes verify the solution, and the new block is added to the chain if it is correct. PoW is resource-intensive and requires significant computational power, which makes it secure but energy-intensive.

PoS, on the other hand, selects block validators based on the amount of cryptocurrency they "stake" or lock up as collateral. Validators are chosen to build new blocks based on their stake, and they have an incentive to perform honestly because any dishonest action could cost them the cryptocurrency they have staked. PoS is more energy-efficient than PoW but relies on the assumption that most validators will act in the network's best interest.

On a blockchain, a user's transaction request is broadcast to all network nodes. Each node receives the transaction and performs initial verification to ensure it is valid and meets specific criteria (e.g., sufficient funds for a cryptocurrency transaction). Once verified, the transaction is placed into a pool of unconfirmed transactions.

Miners (in the case of PoW) or validators (in the case of PoS) then select transactions from the pool to include in the next block. The selection process may depend on factors such as transaction fees or priority. Once a block is formed with a list of transactions, the mining process (PoW) or block validation (PoS) begins.

For PoW, miners compete to find a nonce (a random number) that produces a hash with a specific number of leading zeros when hashed with the block's data. The first miner to find the correct nonce broadcasts the solution to the network. Other nodes verify the solution and, if it is correct, add the new block to their copy of the blockchain. The miner who successfully mined the block is rewarded with a predetermined amount of cryptocurrency, and the process starts again for the next block.

In a PoS system, validators are selected based on their stake in the network before a new block is created. They create the block and broadcast it to the network. Other nodes verify the block's validity and add it to their copy of the blockchain if it is deemed valid. Validators are rewarded with transaction fees from the included transactions and sometimes additional cryptocurrency rewards for their role in maintaining the network's security and integrity.

Occasionally, multiple miners (PoW) or validators (PoS) may simultaneously create valid blocks. This can result in temporary forks, where two or more competing blocks are added to the blockchain at the same height. Eventually, one of the blocks will be accepted by most of the network, becoming the longest chain, while the other competing blocks become stale and discarded.

In PoW, forks can occur when miners find valid blocks at nearly the same time. The network follows the "longest chain" rule, where the chain with the most accumulated proof of work (i.e., the most computational effort invested) is considered the valid chain. The other forks are eventually abandoned, and the network continues with the longest chain.

In PoS, forks are less common but can still occur. Validators may create competing blocks, and the network follows a " finality " rule to determine the valid chain. Finality ensures that validators cannot arbitrarily change their vote, preventing malicious behavior.

The design of blockchain ensures that once a block is added to the chain, it becomes practically immutable. The cryptographic hashes linking blocks together and the consensus mechanism make it extremely difficult to alter past transactions. Any change to data in a block would require the majority of network participants to agree and modify subsequent blocks, which is computationally infeasible.

Due to its immutability, the blockchain is an ideal platform for storing important records like financial transactions, medical information, and legal agreements since it guarantees the integrity of the data stored within. For example, in supply chain management, each step of a product's journey can be recorded on the blockchain, providing an immutable record of its origin, production, and distribution.

Blockchain networks can be categorized into public, private, or consortium blockchains. Anyone can take part in the consensus process and view the entire blockchain on public blockchains like Ethereum and Bitcoin. These networks rely on economic incentives and have robust security due to their decentralized nature.

On the other hand, private blockchains restrict access to approved entities, making them suitable for enterprises and organizations. Private blockchains offer more control over network participants, allowing for faster transaction speeds and scalability. However, they may achieve a different level of decentralization and security than public blockchains.

Consortium blockchains are a hybrid model, where multiple organizations collaborate to operate and maintain the blockchain. These networks combine the advantages of public and private blockchains and are suitable for industries where various stakeholders need to share data and maintain trust.

Blockchain technology offers numerous advantages, including increased transparency, enhanced security, reduced reliance on intermediaries, and improved efficiency in various processes. Decentralization make sure that no single entity controls the data, mitigating the risk of data breaches and unauthorized alterations.

Blockchain can streamline complex processes, such as cross-border payments, supply chain tracking, and smart contracts, by automating them through decentralized applications (dApps). The efficiency and accuracy of blockchain-based systems can lead to cost savings and improved user experiences.

However, blockchain also faces challenges that must be addressed for broader adoption. Scalability remains a significant concern, particularly in public blockchains, where increasing transactions can lead to slower transaction times and higher fees. Efforts are underway to develop solutions such as layer-two scaling solutions and sharding to address scalability concerns.

Environmental issues have been raised by the PoW-based blockchains' energy consumption. As the technology evolves, exploring more energy-efficient consensus mechanisms like PoS becomes crucial for sustainable blockchain growth.

Furthermore, regulatory considerations remain challenging for blockchain adoption, as different jurisdictions have varying approaches to cryptocurrencies and blockchain-based assets. Establishing clear and coherent regulatory frameworks is essential to provide legal certainty and foster responsible innovation in the blockchain space.

Benefits and Limitations of Blockchain

Blockchain technology has become a powerful force for transformation, promising to revolutionize various industries and reshape digital interactions. At its core, blockchain offers a decentralized and immutable ledger that enhances transparency, security, and trust in digital transactions. As this technology gains traction, assessing its potential benefits and inherent limitations is essential.

One of the primary benefits of blockchain is enhanced security and data integrity. Blockchain's cryptographic nature ensures that once data is recorded on the chain, it becomes nearly impossible to alter or delete. Each block's unique hash is linked to the previous block's hash, creating an unbroken chain of transactions. This immutability guarantees data integrity, making blockchain a robust platform for storing critical records, such as financial transactions, medical records, and legal agreements. Blockchain improves security and increases user trust by removing a single point of failure that might allow unwanted changes or data breaches.

Moreover, decentralization lies at the core of blockchain technology, empowering users with direct control over their assets and transactions. Traditional financial systems depend on intermediaries like banks to make transactions possible, which introduces the risk of a failing central authority or malicious behavior. Blockchain eliminates the need for intermediaries, enabling peer-to-peer transactions and reducing costs associated with intermediaries. The trustless nature of blockchain ensures that transactions are validated through consensus mechanisms, making it resistant to fraud and manipulation.

Additionally, blockchain's automated and decentralized nature streamlines complex processes and eliminates manual intervention. Smart contracts, self-executing agreements with predefined terms, enable the automation of various operations without intermediaries. Blockchain, for instance, may follow the flow of goods from manufacture to delivery in real time in the context of supply chain management, thereby minimizing delays, enhancing traceability, and guarding against counterfeiting. These efficiencies can lead to cost savings and enhanced user experiences.

Furthermore, by giving underprivileged communities access to financial services, blockchain technology has the potential to advance financial inclusion. In regions with limited banking infrastructure, individuals can use blockchain-based financial applications to store and transfer funds securely. Additionally, blockchain-based crowdfunding platforms and initial coin offerings (ICOs) offer new avenues for raising capital and funding innovative projects, democratizing access to funding for startups and entrepreneurs.

The transparency blockchain provides is particularly valuable in industries with complex supply chains, where multiple stakeholders can access real-time information about the movement and origin of products. Furthermore, blockchain records' permanent and auditable nature simplifies auditing processes, reducing the need for extensive paperwork and manual verification.

However, blockchain also faces certain limitations that need to be addressed for its broader adoption. Scalability is one of the main difficulties. The network's ability to handle more transactions as they are added to the blockchain may be constrained, resulting in longer transaction times and higher fees. Scalability issues exist for public blockchains like Bitcoin and Ethereum because of the need for all nodes on these decentralized networks to validate transactions. Efforts to address scalability include layer-two solutions like Lightning Network for Bitcoin and Ethereum's transition to Ethereum 2.0 with PoS consensus.

Additionally, blockchain networks that rely on PoW consensus mechanisms, such as Bitcoin, are known for their energy-intensive mining process. The computational power required for mining consumes significant electricity, raising environmental concerns about the carbon footprint of cryptocurrencies. As the demand for blockchain technologies grows, the need to explore more energy-efficient consensus mechanisms, like PoS, becomes crucial for sustainable blockchain growth.

Blockchain and cryptocurrencies' regulatory landscape varies across jurisdictions, leading to regulatory uncertainties for businesses and users. Classifying cryptocurrencies as assets, currencies, or commodities has significant implications for taxation, compliance, and legal requirements. Navigating the diverse regulatory frameworks can be challenging for blockchain-based businesses, potentially hindering innovation and adoption.

While blockchain provides robust security for recorded data, privacy concerns may arise in some cases. Because public blockchains are transparent by design, all network users can see all transactions. While transaction details are encrypted, the associated addresses can be linked to individuals in some situations, compromising anonymity. Efforts to enhance privacy in blockchain include the development of privacy-focused cryptocurrencies and privacy-enhancing technologies like zero-knowledge proofs.

The seamless exchange of data between various blockchain networks is referred to as interoperability. Currently, many blockchain networks operate in isolation, limiting their collaboration and data exchange potential. Achieving interoperability between diverse blockchains is a complex technical challenge that requires standardized protocols and cross-chain communication mechanisms.

In conclusion, blockchain technology presents many benefits, including enhanced security, decentralization, and improved efficiency. Its transparent and immutable nature offers unparalleled trust in digital transactions and data integrity. However, blockchain has challenges like scalability, energy consumption, and regulatory complexities. By addressing these limitations and capitalizing on its benefits, blockchain can revolutionize industries and reshape how we interact with data and conduct business. Responsible adoption, ongoing innovation, and collaboration among stakeholders are crucial for unlocking the full transformative potential of blockchain technology in the digital age.

CHAPTER III

The Birth of Bitcoin

Who Created Bitcoin?

Traditional banking and finance systems have been disrupted by the financial revolution that began with the creation of Bitcoin in 2009. This revolutionary digital currency promised decentralization, transparency, and autonomy from central authorities. Yet, despite its widespread adoption, the identity of Bitcoin's creator remained shrouded in mystery. The enigmatic figure Satoshi Nakamoto introduced the concept of blockchain technology, transforming the world's understanding of finance and technology. In this section, we will explore the origins of Bitcoin, delve into the life and work of Satoshi Nakamoto, and analyze the lasting impact of this anonymous visionary on the world of cryptocurrencies and beyond.

Under the pseudonym Satoshi Nakamoto, a person or group published a whitepaper entitled "Bitcoin: A Peer-to-Peer Electronic Cash System" in a cryptography mailing list in 2008. The whitepaper outlined the framework for a decentralized digital currency that would enable peer-to-peer transactions without the need for intermediaries or central authorities. It introduced the concept of blockchain, a distributed ledger that would record and verify transactions securely and transparently.

In January 2009, Nakamoto mined the first block of the Bitcoin blockchain, also known as the "genesis block." The first-ever Bitcoin transaction happened when Nakamoto transferred 10 bitcoins to computer scientist Hal Finney as a test at this time, marking the network's formal inception.

Despite the profound impact of Bitcoin and Nakamoto's pivotal role in its creation, the true identity of this individual or group has remained a mystery. Satoshi Nakamoto's online presence and interactions were exclusively conducted through cryptography forums, emails, and the Bitcoin Talk forum. There have been numerous speculations and attempts to uncover Nakamoto's identity, but no conclusive evidence has emerged.

Some theories suggest that Nakamoto was a single person, possibly of Japanese origin, given the Japanese name and proficiency in the language displayed in communications. Others propose that Nakamoto may have been a collective effort by a group of developers, given the vast knowledge and expertise demonstrated in creating Bitcoin.

In December 2010, Nakamoto made his final public appearance and handed over the project's development to other prominent figures in the Bitcoin community. Since then, Nakamoto has remained silent, leaving behind an enduring legacy as the enigmatic creator of Bitcoin.

Despite the mystery surrounding Nakamoto's identity, the impact of his creation cannot be overstated. Nakamoto's groundbreaking invention of Bitcoin and the underlying blockchain technology laid the foundation for the proliferation of cryptocurrencies and the rise of decentralized finance (DeFi) platforms.

The concept of a decentralized digital currency addressed long-standing concerns about the inherent flaws of traditional financial systems. By eliminating intermediaries, Bitcoin allows for direct peer-to-peer transactions with reduced fees and greater efficiency. Moreover, as specified in Nakamoto's whitepaper, the limited supply of 21 million bitcoins introduced the concept of scarcity and inflation resistance, positioning Bitcoin as a potential store of value similar to digital gold.

The introduction of blockchain revolutionized data security, integrity, and transparency. Due to the distributed ledger technology utilized by blockchain, it was virtually impossible for hackers to alter the data because transactions were tracked and validated by a network of nodes. This innovation had far-reaching implications beyond finance, leading to its adoption in various industries such as supply chain management, healthcare, and governance.

Bitcoin has become a worldwide phenomenon since Nakamoto faded from view, with a market valuation of several hundred billion dollars. It has garnered widespread adoption, with numerous businesses, merchants, and individuals accepting Bitcoin as payment.

Bitcoin's journey has been challenging and controversial. It has faced criticism for its high energy consumption, particularly in the case of Proof-of-Work (PoW) mining. The scalability debate, centered around Bitcoin's ability to process many transactions per second, has led to forks and the creation of alternative cryptocurrencies like Bitcoin Cash and Bitcoin SV.

Yet, Bitcoin's resilience and enduring popularity have solidified its position as the most dominant cryptocurrency in the market. It continues to attract institutional interest and investment, with major financial institutions offering Bitcoin-related products and services.

Satoshi Nakamoto's decision to withdraw from the public eye raised questions about the motivations behind this anonymity. Some speculate that Nakamoto sought to avoid legal scrutiny or protect his privacy. Others suggest that Nakamoto's anonymity was a deliberate act to ensure the decentralization and security of the Bitcoin network. By remaining anonymous, Nakamoto minimized the risk of becoming a central authority and maintained the network's integrity as a truly decentralized system.

Over the years, numerous individuals have claimed to be Satoshi Nakamoto, but none have provided sufficient evidence to substantiate their claims. The search for Nakamoto has captivated the cryptocurrency community, with some considering the quest to unmask Nakamoto as a futile endeavor that goes against the principles of privacy and decentralization.

The debate around Nakamoto's identity has sparked curiosity and controversy, with some arguing that unmasking Nakamoto would demystify the legend while others believe it could have serious legal and social implications.

How Bitcoin Works

Since the currency's inception in 2009, Bitcoin has gained notoriety and changed the face of both finance and technology. As the first cryptocurrency, Bitcoin introduced the world to blockchain technology, a decentralized and transparent ledger system that enables peer-to-peer transactions without intermediaries. In this section, we will delve into the mechanics of how Bitcoin works, exploring its underlying technology, the process of creating and validating transactions, and the security measures that safeguard the integrity of the network. Understanding the inner workings of Bitcoin is crucial for grasping its potential as a digital currency and its broader implications for the future of finance.

Bitcoin was introduced to the world in 2008 through a whitepaper authored by an individual or group using the pseudonym Satoshi Nakamoto. In a whitepaper known as "Bitcoin: A Peer-to-Peer Electronic Cash System," the essential ideas and workings of Bitcoin were described. The idea of a decentralized digital currency was suggested, one that would run on a network of computers and use blockchain technology to record and verify transactions.

In January 2009, Nakamoto mined the first block of the Bitcoin blockchain, known as the "genesis block." When Nakamoto delivered 10 bitcoins to computer scientist Hal Finney as a test, it was the official beginning of the Bitcoin network and the first-ever Bitcoin transaction.

The foundation of how Bitcoin functions is blockchain technology, a decentralized ledger that records all network transactions. A blockchain is a system of linked blocks, each of which contains a list of confirmed transactions, a timestamp, and a unique number called a cryptographic hash. Each block's hash includes the previous block's hash, creating an unbroken sequence that links all blocks together.

This linking of blocks through cryptographic hashes ensures the immutability of the data recorded on the blockchain. Once a block is added to the chain, it becomes practically impossible to alter past transactions, as any change would require the consensus of most network participants.

Users can create and receive transactions using digital wallets in the Bitcoin network. Two cryptographic keys—a public key (an address) and a private key—make up a Bitcoin wallet. The private key is used for signing and authorizing transactions, while the public key is utilized for receiving funds.

A Bitcoin transaction is broadcast to all network nodes when it is started by a user. Each node examines the sender's funds and the transaction's compliance with the Bitcoin protocol to determine whether the transaction is genuine. If the transaction is valid, it is added to a pool of unconfirmed transactions.

Bitcoin's Proof-of-Work (PoW) consensus mechanism is used to reach consensus and safeguard the network. In Proof of Work, miners compete to figure out difficult mathematical puzzles tied to each block. The network receives the solution from the first miner to arrive at it. Other nodes verify the solution, and the new block is added to the blockchain if it is correct.

Mining serves two primary purposes in the Bitcoin network. Firstly, it verifies and adds new transactions to the blockchain. Second, in order to add new blocks, miners compete with one another and get rewarded with newly created bitcoins and the transaction fees from the added transactions. This reward incentivizes miners to continue securing the network and validating transactions.

To maintain a consistent block creation time, the Bitcoin protocol adjusts the mining difficulty approximately every two weeks. The difficulty level measures the difficulty of finding the correct solution to the mathematical puzzle. If the network's computing power increases, the difficulty level increases to slow down the block creation rate and maintain the average block time of around 10 minutes.

Conversely, if the network's computing power decreases, the difficulty level decreases to speed up the block creation rate. This dynamic adjustment ensures that new blocks are added to the blockchain at a relatively consistent rate, regardless of fluctuations in network participation.

Nodes play a crucial role in the Bitcoin network. Each node is a computer that participates in validating and relaying transactions across the network. Nodes keep a copy of the whole blockchain and confirm that new transactions and blocks are genuine.

Full nodes validate transactions and blocks by independently checking the rules of the Bitcoin protocol. If a transaction or block does not comply with the rules, it is rejected by the node. This decentralized validation process ensures the integrity and security of the network, as transactions must meet consensus rules to be considered valid.

One of the critical challenges that Bitcoin addresses is the double-spending problem. In traditional electronic payment systems, a digital asset can be replicated and spent more than once. To prevent double spending, Bitcoin uses the blockchain and PoW consensus mechanism to reach consensus on the order of transactions.

The Byzantine Generals Problem is a theoretical scenario that describes the challenge of reaching consensus among distributed participants with the presence of faulty nodes. In the context of Bitcoin, this problem is solved through the decentralized and trustless nature of the network. The consensus mechanism ensures that all nodes agree on the validity of transactions, preventing double spending and securing the network against malicious attacks.

Bitcoin's security is ensured by the decentralized nature of the network and the robustness of the PoW consensus mechanism. The sheer computational power required to alter the blockchain makes it economically infeasible for malicious actors to manipulate the network.

While Bitcoin transactions are pseudonymous, meaning that they are linked to addresses rather than personal identities, the public nature of the blockchain raises privacy concerns. Although transaction details are encrypted, it is still possible for individuals to link addresses to real-world identities in some cases. Various techniques and technologies, such as coin mixing and privacy-focused cryptocurrencies, have been developed to enhance privacy in Bitcoin transactions.

Throughout Bitcoin's history, there have been instances of forks, where the blockchain splits into two separate chains with different consensus rules. Forks can be intentional upgrades to the protocol or unintended consequences of disagreements among network participants.

Soft forks are backward-compatible upgrades to the protocol, while hard forks introduce new rules incompatible with the previous version. In the case of a hard fork, two chains diverge, and network participants must choose which chain to follow.

In conclusion, Bitcoin's revolutionary impact on the world of finance and technology is a testament to the genius of its enigmatic creator, Satoshi Nakamoto. By introducing blockchain technology and a decentralized digital currency, Nakamoto laid the groundwork for a paradigm shift in how we perceive money, transactions, and trust.

The Significance of Bitcoin

Bitcoin, the first and most prominent cryptocurrency, has ushered in a new era of finance and technology, disrupting traditional financial systems and challenging the status quo. Since the introduction of Bitcoin in 2009, it has grown into a global phenomenon, gaining widespread adoption and sparking a wave of innovation in the field of blockchain technology. In this section, we will explore the significance of Bitcoin, examining its impact on financial autonomy, its potential as a store of value, its role in promoting financial inclusion, and its broader implications for the future of the global economy.

One of the most significant aspects of Bitcoin is its promise of financial autonomy and empowerment. Traditional financial systems are often centralized, with banks and financial institutions serving as intermediaries that control access to funds and oversee transactions. This centralization can lead to censorship, data breaches, and high transaction fees.

On the other hand, Bitcoin operates on a decentralized network of computers, where transactions are verified by a distributed network of nodes rather than a central authority. This decentralization ensures that individuals have direct control over their funds and transactions, free from interference or censorship by any single entity. Individuals may perform peer-to-peer transactions using Bitcoin due to its decentralized structure, which removes the need for middlemen and lowers transaction costs.

Bitcoin's limited supply and scarcity have positioned it as a potential store of value, comparable to digital gold. Satoshi Nakamoto's whitepaper specified a maximum supply of 21 million bitcoins, creating a deflationary asset with a predictable issuance rate. In contrast with typical fiat currencies, which are susceptible to inflation as a result of central bank policy, this currency has a set supply.

The idea of Bitcoin as digital gold gained traction as investors sought a hedge against economic uncertainty and inflation. Like gold, Bitcoin is considered a non-correlated asset, meaning its value is not directly tied to the performance of traditional financial markets. As a result, some individuals view Bitcoin as a safe-haven asset that can preserve value during economic downturns and provide a store of wealth in times of uncertainty.

By giving unbanked and underbanked communities access to financial services, Bitcoin has the potential to support financial inclusion. In regions with limited banking infrastructure, individuals can use Bitcoin as a secure and accessible alternative to traditional banking. All that is required is a mobile phone or an internet connection, allowing even those without a formal bank account to participate in the global economy.

Furthermore, Bitcoin enables cross-border transactions without the need for expensive remittance services or foreign exchange fees. This functionality has significant implications for people who depend on remittances from family members who work abroad because Bitcoin provides a quicker and more efficient way to transmit funds.

In countries experiencing hyperinflation or economic instability, citizens often face the erosion of their purchasing power and the devaluation of their local currency. In such circumstances, Bitcoin can offer a form of financial sovereignty and protection against the devaluation of national currencies.

Citizens of countries with volatile economies have turned to Bitcoin to preserve wealth and shield themselves from the adverse effects of hyperinflation. The ability to store value in a deflationary asset like Bitcoin can provide individuals with financial security in uncertain economic environments.

Beyond its role as a digital currency, Bitcoin's creation introduced the world to blockchain technology, a transformative innovation with far-reaching implications. Blockchain technology is a decentralized, open-source ledger system that securely and irrevocably records and validates transactions.

Blockchain technology has been used in several areas since Bitcoin's introduction, namely supply chain management, healthcare, real estate, and government. Its ability to streamline complex processes, increase transparency, and reduce the reliance on intermediaries has attracted the attention of businesses and governments.

Despite its numerous advantages, Bitcoin also faces challenges and criticisms. While offering significant benefits, its decentralized nature can make it susceptible to volatility and price fluctuations. Investors and regulators are both concerned about the lack of regulatory monitoring and the existence of fraudulent schemes.

The energy-intensive mining process, particularly in Proof-of-Work (PoW) consensus mechanisms, has drawn criticism for its environmental impact. Efforts to explore more energy-efficient consensus mechanisms, such as Proof-of-Stake (PoS), are ongoing to address this concern.

As Bitcoin's popularity and price have surged, it has attracted significant attention from investors and speculators. While some view Bitcoin as a long-term investment and hedge against economic uncertainty, others approach it as a speculative asset, aiming to profit from price fluctuations.

The volatility of Bitcoin's price has both attracted and deterred potential investors. The value of Bitcoin has experienced significant swings, ranging from rapid growth to steep corrections. This volatility can create profit opportunities but also entails significant risks.

The significance of Bitcoin lies not only in its present impact but also in its potential to shape the future of global finance. As the first cryptocurrency, Bitcoin has paved the way for the emergence of thousands of other cryptocurrencies and blockchain projects.

Blockchain innovations and the continuous development of Bitcoin have the potential to completely transform financial systems, speed up cross-border transactions, and promote financial inclusion on a global scale. Additionally, as regulatory frameworks evolve and mature, Bitcoin's integration into traditional financial systems may increase, potentially influencing monetary policies and international trade.

CHAPTER IV

Exploring Other
Major Cryptocurrencies

Ethereum

Ethereum, introduced in 2015 by Vitalik Buterin, has become a groundbreaking platform in blockchain technology. Building on the principles of Bitcoin, Ethereum enabled the establishment of smart contracts and decentralized apps (dApps), expanding blockchain's potential beyond just digital currency. In this section, we will delve into the mechanics of Ethereum, exploring its underlying technology, the significance of smart contracts, the rise of decentralized applications, and the potential implications of this revolutionary platform on the future of the internet and beyond.

Ethereum emerged due to Vitalik Buterin's vision to enhance the functionality of blockchain technology. In late 2013, Buterin published the Ethereum whitepaper, outlining a decentralized platform that could execute smart contracts and dApps. The concept gained traction, and in mid-2014, Buterin and a team of co-founders launched a crowdfunding campaign that raised over $18 million in Bitcoin to fund the development of Ethereum.

The first block, or the "genesis block," was mined on July 30, 2015, when Ethereum's blockchain became live. Ethereum's native cryptocurrency, Ether (ETH), is used to power the platform, acting as both a digital currency and fuel for executing smart contracts.

At the core of Ethereum's functionality lies the Ethereum Virtual Machine (EVM). The EVM is a Turing-complete virtual machine, which means it can execute any program given enough time and resources. This flexibility enables developers to write and deploy smart contracts, self-executing agreements with predefined conditions and outcomes.

Smart contracts are coded in high-level programming languages like Solidity and Vyper, making them accessible to developers with different backgrounds. Once deployed on the Ethereum blockchain, smart contracts are immutable and autonomously executed when triggered by specific conditions.

Smart contracts represent one of Ethereum's most significant contributions to the world of blockchain technology. These self-executing contracts automate the enforcement of terms and conditions, removing the need for intermediaries in contractual agreements. Smart contracts can be used to facilitate various transactions, such as crowdfunding campaigns (Initial Coin Offerings or ICOs), supply chain management, decentralized finance (DeFi) protocols, and more.

The automation and transparency of smart contracts enhance trust among parties, as the contract's execution is visible on the public blockchain. Moreover, blockchain technology ensures that the contract terms cannot be altered or tampered with once deployed, providing an immutable record of the agreement.

Ethereum's capabilities extend beyond digital currency and smart contracts, facilitating the development of decentralized applications or dApps. An application known as a "dApp" runs on a decentralized network and makes use of blockchain technology for data storage, security, and execution.

dApps are more resistant to failures and censorship since they operate on a distributed network of nodes rather than traditional applications, which rely on centralized servers. DApps can be built for various purposes, including financial services, gaming, social media, identity verification, etc.

The development of dApps has opened up new avenues for innovation and entrepreneurship, as developers can create applications without needing a central authority's approval. However, the user experience and scalability of dApps remain challenges that developers continue to address.

Initially, Ethereum operated on a Proof-of-Work (PoW) consensus mechanism similar to Bitcoin. However, Ethereum has been transitioning to a more energy-efficient and scalable consensus mechanism known as Proof-of-Stake (PoS). Based on the number of tokens that validators, or stakers, have and are prepared to "stake" as collateral, PoS enables them to build new blocks as well as validate transactions.

The shift to PoS is part of Ethereum's ongoing upgrade known as Ethereum 2.0, aimed at improving the network's scalability, security, and energy efficiency. By reducing the need for energy-intensive mining, PoS seeks to address concerns about the environmental impact of blockchain networks.

One of Ethereum's most significant use cases is the rise of decentralized finance (DeFi) applications. Without the need of conventional financial intermediaries, DeFi platforms use smart contracts to offer financial services. These services include lending and borrowing, yield farming, decentralized exchanges (DEXs), stablecoins, and more.

DeFi has experienced explosive growth, attracting billions of dollars in total value locked (TVL) within these platforms. DeFi protocols aim to democratize access to financial services, enabling users worldwide to access lending and investment opportunities without going through traditional financial institutions.

While Ethereum has achieved significant milestones, it faces challenges primarily related to scalability. The increased number of users and transactions has put pressure on the network, leading to high gas fees and slower transaction times. Ethereum 2.0, with its shift to PoS and the introduction of shard chains, aims to address these scalability issues and increase the network's capacity.

Interoperability is another challenge faced by Ethereum and the broader blockchain ecosystem. The expansion and usability of the ecosystem depend on maintaining seamless data exchange and connectivity between multiple networks as more blockchains and decentralized applications are built.

A broad and enthusiastic community of researchers, developers, enthusiasts, and users are responsible for Ethereum's development and governance. Ethereum Improvement Proposals (EIPs) allow the community to propose and discuss changes to the Ethereum protocol. Major decisions, such as upgrades and network functionality changes, are determined through a community consensus process.

Ethereum's potential extends beyond finance and technology, with implications for various aspects of society. The transparency and immutability of the blockchain have applications in supply chain management, voting systems, intellectual property rights, and identity verification.

However, with new possibilities come ethical considerations. Privacy concerns, the potential for misuse of smart contracts, and the impact of blockchain technology on social structures and governance systems raise important questions that society must grapple with.

Ripple (XRP)

Ripple (XRP) is a revolutionary digital payment protocol that has emerged as a disruptor in cross-border transactions and remittances. Created by Ripple Labs in 2012, XRP aims to provide fast, cost-effective, and secure cross-border payment solutions by leveraging blockchain technology and a unique consensus mechanism. In this section, we will delve into the mechanics of Ripple (XRP), explore its role in the global financial landscape, examine its use cases beyond cross-border payments, and analyze its potential implications for the future of the financial industry.

Ripple Labs, a San Francisco-based fintech company, developed the Ripple protocol and its native digital asset, XRP. Launched in 2012, Ripple aimed to address the inefficiencies and delays in cross-border transactions prevalent in traditional banking systems.

Unlike other cryptocurrencies, XRP is not based on Proof-of-Work (PoW) or Proof-of-Stake (PoS) consensus mechanisms. Instead, it employs a unique consensus algorithm called the Ripple Protocol Consensus Algorithm (RPCA), allowing faster and more cost-effective transactions.

At the core of Ripple's ecosystem is the XRP Ledger, a decentralized blockchain that serves as the infrastructure for cross-border payments. The XRP Ledger enables the issuance, transfer, and settlement of XRP, providing a secure and transparent platform for financial transactions.

The Ripple network connects financial institutions and payment providers through a decentralized network of nodes. These nodes maintain the XRP Ledger and participate in the consensus process, reaching an agreement on the order and validity of transactions without relying on energy-intensive mining.

One of Ripple's primary use cases is transforming cross-border payments and remittances. Traditional international money transfers often suffer from high fees, delays, and the need for multiple intermediaries, resulting in an inefficient and costly process.

Ripple's technology enables real-time settlement of cross-border payments, significantly reducing transaction times and costs. Financial institutions and payment providers can use XRP as a bridge currency to facilitate instant currency conversions, eliminating the need for multiple intermediate currencies and reducing foreign exchange fees.

The efficiency and cost-effectiveness of Ripple's cross-border payment solutions have attracted partnerships with major banks and financial institutions worldwide. Ripple's payment solutions are designed to complement existing banking systems and provide a more seamless and competitive alternative for international transactions.

Ripple's focus on improving cross-border payments also has implications for financial inclusion. Traditional banking systems often exclude individuals in underbanked and developing regions from accessing affordable and efficient cross-border payment services.

Through Ripple's platform, individuals in these regions can access fast and cost-effective remittance services. Reduced transaction fees and improved transaction speed can empower individuals and businesses in underserved areas, facilitating more significant participation in the global economy.

Ripple's global payment network, known as RippleNet, comprises a growing network of financial institutions and payment service providers. RippleNet allows participants to connect and transact with each other seamlessly, promoting interoperability and facilitating cross-border payments.

Ripple envisions a concept known as the "Internet of Value," where the movement of money is as fluid and efficient as the transfer of information on the Internet. By enabling direct, frictionless, and real-time transfers of value, Ripple aims to build a borderless and interconnected financial ecosystem.

Beyond its utility in cross-border payments, XRP is a digital asset with distinct features. XRP has a limited supply, with a maximum of 100 billion tokens in existence. Unlike Bitcoin and other cryptocurrencies, XRP's total supply was pre-mined at its creation, with a significant portion held by Ripple Labs.

Critics have raised concerns about XRP's centralization due to the concentration of tokens held by Ripple Labs. However, Ripple has taken steps to promote the decentralization of the XRP Ledger, encouraging greater participation from independent validators.

Ripple has faced regulatory challenges in various jurisdictions due to its unique digital asset and payment protocol status. The distinction between XRP as a digital currency and Ripple's role as a company has been a subject of legal scrutiny.

Some regulators have classified XRP as a security, while others consider it a commodity. The regulatory environment surrounding cryptocurrencies remains complex and varies across different countries, adding uncertainty to the adoption and use of XRP.

Ripple has also explored partnerships with central banks to explore the use of XRP for central bank digital currencies (CBDCs). Integrating XRP into CBDCs could enhance cross-border interoperability and facilitate efficient settlement between different fiat currencies.

In a rapidly evolving blockchain and cryptocurrency landscape, interoperability between different protocols and networks becomes crucial. Ripple has actively promoted collaboration and open standards in the industry, seeking to establish a more interconnected and efficient financial ecosystem.

Litecoin

Litecoin, often called "digital silver," is a pioneering cryptocurrency created by Charlie Lee in 2011. Litecoin was created to deal with some of the perceived drawbacks of Bitcoin, including transaction speed and scalability. It is positioned to serve as peer-to-peer digital currency. Over the years, Litecoin has gained popularity as a reliable and efficient digital asset, earning its place as one of the leading cryptocurrencies in the market. In this section, we will delve into the mechanics of Litecoin, explore its key differentiators, analyze its role in the cryptocurrency ecosystem, and assess its potential implications for the future of finance and digital currencies.

Litecoin was introduced to the world on October 7, 2011, by Charlie Lee, a former Google engineer. Inspired by Bitcoin's success, Lee sought to create a digital currency that could complement Bitcoin's digital gold narrative. The name "Litecoin" reflects its intention to be a lightweight, faster, and more efficient version of Bitcoin.

Like Bitcoin, Litecoin runs on a decentralized blockchain and is based on an open-source technology. It shares many similarities with Bitcoin, but its key differentiators lie in its block generation time, total supply, and mining algorithm.

Litecoin employs a different mining algorithm than Bitcoin, known as Scrypt. Scrypt is designed to be more memory-intensive, making it less susceptible to the application-specific integrated circuits (ASICs) used in Bitcoin mining. As a result, Litecoin's mining process remains accessible to individual miners using consumer-grade hardware, promoting decentralization.

The Scrypt algorithm also allows for faster block generation times, reducing the average time to produce a new block from 10 minutes (Bitcoin's block time) to approximately 2.5 minutes in Litecoin. This faster block generation enables speedier transaction confirmations, making Litecoin a more suitable option for day-to-day transactions.

Litecoin's faster block generation time contributes to its advantage in transaction speeds over Bitcoin. In a scenario where both blockchains experience the same transaction volume, Litecoin can process more transactions in a given timeframe due to its shorter block time.

This faster transaction speed has made Litecoin a preferred choice for specific use cases, such as retail payments and point-of-sale transactions. However, it is essential to note that Litecoin's transaction speed is still significantly slower than traditional payment systems like credit card networks.

In May 2017, Litecoin became the first major cryptocurrency to activate Segregated Witness (SegWit), a protocol upgrade aimed at improving transaction processing efficiency. SegWit separates the transaction signature data from the transaction data, increasing the capacity of each block and reducing transaction fees.

The activation of SegWit on the Litecoin network allowed for a more significant number of transactions to be processed within a single block, improving the overall scalability of the network. The successful implementation of SegWit on Litecoin has also influenced other cryptocurrencies to adopt the upgrade.

As a testament to its commitment to interoperability and collaboration within the cryptocurrency space, Litecoin was among the first cryptocurrencies to enable atomic swaps. Atomic swaps allow for direct peer-to-peer exchange of cryptocurrencies without intermediaries or exchanges.

Furthermore, Litecoin has also integrated with the Lightning Network, a second-layer scaling solution that enables fast and low-cost transactions on top of the main Litecoin blockchain. The Lightning Network enhances the scalability of Litecoin, facilitating micropayments and making it more suitable for everyday transactions.

Litecoin's positioning as the "digital silver" is an acknowledgment of its complementary relationship with Bitcoin. While Bitcoin is often seen as a store of value or digital gold, Litecoin aims to serve as a practical and efficient medium of exchange.

The concept of digital silver reflects Litecoin's utility in facilitating day-to-day transactions and smaller value transfers, whereas Bitcoin is perceived as a long-term investment or a means of preserving wealth. Combining cryptocurrencies in an investor's portfolio offers diverse exposure to the cryptocurrency market.

Litecoin has achieved significant adoption and recognition in the cryptocurrency community. It is widely traded on various cryptocurrency exchanges, making it easily accessible to investors and users worldwide.

Additionally, Litecoin has been integrated into various payment platforms and businesses, enabling users to spend LTC for goods and services. Its acceptance by merchants and retailers further enhances its utility as a medium of exchange.

While Litecoin has gained a strong foothold in the cryptocurrency market, it also faces challenges and potential limitations. One significant challenge is the competition from other cryptocurrencies that offer similar features, including faster transaction speeds and lower fees.

Moreover, the ongoing evolution of the cryptocurrency landscape, technological advancements, and changes in market sentiment may influence Litecoin's market position and adoption in the future.

Litecoin's contributions to the cryptocurrency ecosystem extend beyond its role as a digital currency. Its successful activation of SegWit and integration with the Lightning Network has influenced the development of scaling solutions for other cryptocurrencies.

Because of its focus on decentralization and dedication to cooperation and interoperability, Litecoin has the potential to be a key player in the development of international finance and the widespread adoption of blockchain technology.

Bitcoin Cash

Bitcoin Cash, often called BCH, emerged as a significant fork of Bitcoin in 2017, seeking to address the scalability limitations of the original cryptocurrency. A group of developers and miners created Bitcoin Cash to increase the block size, allowing for more significant transaction throughput and lower fees. Since its inception, Bitcoin Cash has positioned itself as a peer-to-peer electronic cash system focusing on fast and affordable transactions. In this section, we will explore the mechanics of Bitcoin Cash, analyze its critical differentiators from Bitcoin, evaluate its adoption and use cases, and discuss its potential implications for the future of digital cash and the broader cryptocurrency ecosystem.

On August 1, 2017, the network that holds Bitcoin underwent a contentious hard fork that gave rise to Bitcoin Cash. The fork was started as a result of an ongoing discussion on the scalability and speed of transactions of the original Bitcoin network within the Bitcoin community.

The main point of contention revolved around Bitcoin's block size, which was capped at 1 megabyte (MB). This limitation led to increasing transaction fees and longer confirmation times during periods of high network activity. As a solution, a group of developers and miners proposed increasing the block size to 8 MB, eventually creating Bitcoin Cash.

Bitcoin Cash shares many similarities with its parent cryptocurrency, Bitcoin's decentralized nature, Proof-of-Work (PoW) consensus mechanism, and fixed supply of 21 million coins. However, several key differences set Bitcoin Cash apart:

One of the most significant differences is Bitcoin Cash's larger block size, initially set at 8 MB and later increased further through network upgrades. This larger block size allows Bitcoin Cash to process more transactions per block, increasing transaction throughput and reducing transaction fees.

With its larger block size, Bitcoin Cash can accommodate more transactions in each block, leading to faster confirmation times than Bitcoin. The faster transaction speed enhances its suitability as a medium of exchange for everyday transactions.

Bitcoin Cash utilizes the "Emergency Difficulty Adjustment" (EDA) algorithm to adjust mining difficulty dynamically. This adjustment mechanism ensures a more stable block production rate, preventing long periods between blocks during reduced mining activity.

Since its creation, Bitcoin Cash has gained traction as a digital cash system focusing on peer-to-peer transactions. Its ability to process larger blocks and faster transactions has made it attractive for merchants and businesses looking to accept digital payments.

Bitcoin Cash has seen adoption in various industries, including e-commerce, online gaming, and remittance services. It is practical for micropayments and frequent transactions due to its lower transaction fees and quicker confirmation times.

Some Bitcoin Cash supporters also encourage its adoption in areas with insufficient access to conventional banking institutions. Its potential to provide a more affordable and efficient payment system could promote financial inclusion and empower individuals with greater control over their finances.

The split in the cryptocurrency community was another effect of the hard fork that produced Bitcoin Cash. While some supporters believed that Bitcoin Cash offered a practical solution to Bitcoin's scalability issues, others viewed it as a contentious and unnecessary fork.

The split led to divisions between the Bitcoin and Bitcoin Cash communities, with both camps advocating their respective cryptocurrencies. As a result, the two networks have developed independently, with different development teams, upgrade paths, and visions for the future.

Similar to Bitcoin, Bitcoin Cash is constantly being updated and improved to increase its use and scalability. These upgrades address various aspects, including network security, transaction efficiency, and user experience.

Bitcoin Cash developers are actively exploring solutions to increase further block sizes, such as the Gigablock Testnet Initiative and proposals for flexible block sizes. These initiatives seek to achieve even higher transaction throughput while maintaining network security and decentralization.

Bitcoin Cash's focus on scalability and fast, low-cost transactions positions it as a viable digital cash solution in the cryptocurrency ecosystem. Its potential to facilitate day-to-day transactions and micropayments has attracted merchants, businesses, and individuals seeking an alternative to traditional payment systems.

Furthermore, its emphasis on practical use cases aligns with the original vision of Bitcoin as peer-to-peer electronic cash. However, the competitive landscape of cryptocurrencies remains dynamic, and Bitcoin Cash faces competition from other digital assets that also aim to address scalability and transaction speed challenges.

Despite its unique features and potential, Bitcoin Cash has faced criticisms and challenges. Some critics argue that its focus on increasing block size may compromise network security and decentralization in the long run. Additionally, the contentious nature of its fork and the split in the community have also been subjects of criticism.

Moreover, Bitcoin Cash faces competition from other cryptocurrencies that offer similar features, such as faster transaction speeds and lower fees. Staying competitive and relevant as the cryptocurrency market evolves requires continuous development and innovation.

As cryptocurrencies continue to evolve, digital cash solutions like Bitcoin Cash will play a pivotal role in shaping the future of finance.

The growing interest in digital currencies and the demand for fast and cost-effective transactions suggest a promising future for Bitcoin Cash and similar cryptocurrencies.

The development and adoption of Layer 2 scaling solutions, such as the Lightning Network, further complement Bitcoin Cash's functionality and enhance its scalability.

Adopting digital cash solutions like Bitcoin Cash faces regulatory challenges in various jurisdictions. Governments and financial regulators are still developing frameworks and guidelines for cryptocurrencies, which can influence their acceptance and usage.

Moreover, merchant adoption and integration into traditional payment systems remain crucial for the broader adoption of Bitcoin Cash. As more merchants and businesses embrace digital cash solutions, the use of Bitcoin Cash for everyday transactions may become more widespread.

Other Prominent Cryptocurrencies

While Bitcoin and Ethereum dominate the headlines in the cryptocurrency world, the broader landscape is teeming with many innovative digital assets, each offering unique features and use cases. These cryptocurrencies, often called altcoins, have emerged as alternatives and complements to the pioneering cryptocurrencies. In this section, we will explore a selection of other prominent cryptocurrencies, shedding light on their features, use cases, and contributions to the evolving blockchain ecosystem. From privacy-focused coins to decentralized finance (DeFi) platforms and beyond, the diverse array of cryptocurrencies showcases the boundless possibilities that blockchain technology has unleashed.

Cardano is a blockchain platform that emphasizes scientific research and peer-reviewed academic papers in its development. Founded by Charles Hoskinson, a co-founder of Ethereum, Cardano aims to build a more secure and sustainable blockchain infrastructure through its layered architecture. The platform is designed to facilitate smart contracts, decentralized applications (dApps), and real-world use cases. Cardano's focus on formal verification and transparent governance has garnered attention, positioning it as a contender in the competitive world of blockchain platforms.

Polkadot is a multi-chain blockchain platform designed to enable interoperability between different blockchains. Founded by Dr. Gavin Wood, a co-founder of Ethereum, Polkadot seeks to address the issue of blockchain fragmentation by allowing multiple blockchains to connect and share information seamlessly. This interoperability enables data transfer, asset exchange, and other cross-chain functionalities, making Polkadot an essential player in the evolution of the internet of blockchains.

Chainlink is a decentralized oracle network that facilitates smart contracts interacting with real-world data and external systems. Oracles are crucial in bringing off-chain data onto the blockchain, enabling smart contracts to execute based on real-time information. As smart contracts continue to gain traction in various industries, Chainlink's robust oracle infrastructure becomes increasingly vital for connecting blockchain applications with real-world data and events.

Monero is a privacy-focused cryptocurrency that prioritizes user anonymity and fungibility. Monero makes sure that transactions are hidden and unlinkable with the use of its ring signature and stealth address technologies, making it challenging to track the movement of funds. These privacy features have attracted users seeking enhanced confidentiality and have positioned Monero as a significant player in privacy-focused cryptocurrencies.

Uniswap is a decentralized exchange (DEX) protocol built on the Ethereum blockchain. As part of the DeFi ecosystem, Uniswap enables users to swap and trade various tokens directly from their wallets without intermediaries or centralized exchanges. Its automated market-making (AMM) mechanism allows users to provide liquidity to pools and earn rewards. Uniswap's user-friendly and decentralized nature has contributed to its popularity within the DeFi space.

Binance Coin, native to the Binance exchange, initially served as a utility token for reduced trading fees on the platform. However, Binance has evolved into much more, including a core Binance Smart Chain (BSC) component. As BSC gains popularity, BNB's utility and demand have surged. BNB is now used for transactions, DeFi applications, and participating in token sales on the Binance Launchpad. Binance Coin's utility and the Binance ecosystem's growth have solidified its place as a significant player in the cryptocurrency market.

Stellar is a blockchain platform that facilitates cross-border payments and seamless asset transfers. Its focus on financial inclusion and serving the unbanked population has attracted partnerships with various organizations and financial institutions. Stellar's unique consensus algorithm and distributed exchange make it an attractive option for efficient cross-border transactions and the tokenization of assets.

Solana is a high-performance blockchain platform built for scalability and fast transaction speeds. Solana intends to perform thousands of transactions for each second without compromising security by utilizing its Proof-of-History (PoH) consensus mechanism. As the demand for scalable and decentralized applications continues to grow, Solana's technological advancements and focus on user experience have positioned it as a prominent player in the blockchain ecosystem.

EOS is a blockchain platform known for its high throughput and scalability, aiming to support a wide range of decentralized applications. Its delegated Proof-of-Stake (dPoS) consensus mechanism allows for fast block confirmation times and reduced energy consumption. EOS's focus on developer-friendly tools and resources has attracted a vibrant community of developers building diverse applications on the platform.

The blockchain platform VeChain focuses on managing and tracing supply chains. It aims to enhance transparency and trust in supply chains by enabling the tracking and verification of products from the source to the end consumer. VeChain's combination of blockchain technology, Internet of Things (IoT) integration, and real-world use cases has attracted partnerships with various industries, such as luxury goods, food safety, and healthcare.

Tezos is a self-amending blockchain platform that allows stakeholders to participate in the governance and evolution of the network. Through its on-chain governance model, Tezos can upgrade and improve itself without requiring hard forks. Its focus on security, formal verification, and sustainability has garnered interest from developers and enterprises seeking a robust and stable blockchain platform.

Initially created as a meme coin, Dogecoin has evolved into a widely recognized digital asset with a large and passionate community. Despite its lighthearted origins, Dogecoin's low transaction fees and fast confirmation times have positioned it as a practical option for small-value transactions and tipping on social media platforms. Its strong community support and charitable initiatives have made Dogecoin a unique player in the cryptocurrency ecosystem.

The cryptocurrency landscape is a dynamic and ever-evolving ecosystem, with many prominent cryptocurrencies contributing to its diversity and innovation. From fast and scalable blockchains to privacy-focused coins and DeFi platforms, each digital asset offers unique features and serves specific use cases.

CHAPTER V

How to Buy and
Store Cryptocurrencies

Choosing a Cryptocurrency Exchange

As the popularity of cryptocurrencies surges, the need for secure and efficient cryptocurrency exchanges has become increasingly apparent. Cryptocurrency exchanges act as gateways to the digital asset world, facilitating the buying, selling, and trading of various cryptocurrencies. However, with many exchanges available, selecting the right one can take time and effort for newcomers and seasoned investors. This section will delve into the essential factors to consider when choosing a cryptocurrency exchange. From security and user experience to trading fees and supported assets, understanding these crucial aspects will empower users to make informed decisions and find the most suitable platform for their needs.

The first and foremost consideration when choosing a cryptocurrency exchange is security. Given cryptocurrencies' decentralized and pseudonymous nature, the risk of hacking and fraud is ever-present. Therefore, it is crucial to select an exchange that prioritizes security measures.

Look for exchanges implementing industry-standard security protocols such as two-factor authentication (2FA), cold storage for funds, and encryption for user data. Additionally, check whether the exchange complies with relevant regulations in your jurisdiction. Regulatory compliance can enhance trust and transparency, as exchanges adhering to compliance standards are more likely to follow best security and customer protection practices.

Research the reputation of the cryptocurrency exchange before creating an account. Seek feedback from other users and read reviews on reputable websites or forums. A positive track record of reliability, customer support, and prompt issue resolution is essential for a trustworthy exchange. Conversely, a history of security breaches or unresolved customer complaints should raise red flags.

A cryptocurrency exchange's user experience and interface can significantly impact trading efficiency and ease of use. Look for exchanges with intuitive and user-friendly interfaces and comprehensive trading tools and charts. A well-designed platform can enhance your trading experience and reduce the risk of costly errors.

Not all cryptocurrency exchanges support the same range of cryptocurrencies and trading pairs. If you have a specific cryptocurrency or altcoin in mind, ensure that the exchange supports it. Additionally, check the available trading pairs to ensure you can quickly execute the desired trades.

Liquidity is a crucial factor in a cryptocurrency exchange. An exchange with high liquidity allows for faster order execution and tighter bid-ask spreads, ensuring you can enter or exit positions with minimal slippage. High liquidity is significant for large trades and for trading less popular or lower market cap cryptocurrencies.

Trading fees can significantly impact your trading profitability, especially if you are a frequent trader. Different exchanges have varying fee structures, including maker and taker, withdrawal, and deposit fees. Carefully review the fee schedule and choose an exchange with transparent and competitive rates that align with your trading style and volume.

In the fast-paced world of cryptocurrencies, efficient customer support is essential. Look for exchanges with responsive customer service that can address your queries and resolve issues promptly. The availability of multiple support channels, such as email, live chat, and phone support, can also be a decisive factor.

Check the available payment methods for depositing and withdrawing funds on the exchange. Credit/debit cards, bank transfers, and e-wallets are just a few of the fiat currencies and methods of payment that are supported by different exchanges. Choose an exchange that aligns with your preferred payment method and currency.

Some cryptocurrency exchanges have geographic restrictions and may not be available in all countries. Ensure that the exchange is accessible in your region before creating an account.

Many exchanges enforce Know Your Customer (KYC) and identity verification procedures to comply with anti-money laundering (AML) regulations. Be prepared to provide identification documents and undergo verification if required. Remember that exchanges with robust KYC procedures often offer an added layer of security and may be more trustworthy.

A mobile app can be a valuable feature for traders on the go. Verify that the exchange has a mobile app that is appropriate for your device and operating system. You are able to manage and keep an eye on your trades using a mobile app, which offers flexibility and convenience.

Thoroughly research the background and history of the exchange. Look for details such as the year of establishment, the team behind the exchange, and any notable partnerships. A well-established exchange with a strong team and a history of successful operations can provide added confidence in its reliability and security.

Some cryptocurrency exchanges offer insurance coverage for user funds, protecting against losses due to hacking or security breaches. While not all exchanges provide this feature, it can be an added layer of protection for your assets.

Consider whether the exchange offers educational resources and tools to help users stay informed and make informed trading decisions. Exchanges with educational content, market analysis, and trading guides can be beneficial, especially for beginners.

For novice traders or those exploring new strategies, an exchange that offers a demo trading or test environment can be advantageous. With this function, you can develop confidence and experience by practicing trading without using actual funds before engaging in live trading.

Exchanges operating in a regulated environment may provide additional confidence and security. Look for exchanges that comply with relevant regulatory frameworks and maintain operational transparency.

Anyone joining the world of digital assets must take the essential step of selecting the best cryptocurrency exchange. Users may find the best exchange to fulfill their unique needs and preferences by looking at aspects like security, user experience, fees, supported cryptocurrency, liquidity, and customer service.

Setting Up a Wallet

A wallet is the gateway to managing and safeguarding your digital assets in cryptocurrencies. A cryptocurrency wallet is not a physical object but rather a software application or a hardware device that enables users to store, send, and receive various cryptocurrencies securely. As the popularity of cryptocurrencies continues to grow, understanding how to set up and use a wallet becomes paramount for anyone looking to participate in this decentralized financial revolution. This section will explore the different types of cryptocurrency wallets, the steps involved in setting up a wallet, the importance of security measures, and best practices for managing your digital assets.

Cryptocurrency wallets come in various forms, each with advantages and security considerations. Understanding the different types of wallets is crucial before deciding on the most suitable option. Physical objects called hardware wallets are made for offline cryptocurrency storage. They provide an extra layer of security by keeping private keys offline, reducing the risk of online hacking attempts. Ledger, Trezor, and KeepKey are some of the well-known hardware wallets. On the other hand, software wallets come in different varieties, such as desktop wallets, mobile wallets, and web wallets. Desktop wallets are computer programs that you may install and use to manage your private keys completely. Mobile wallets, designed for smartphones and tablets, provide portability and convenience for day-to-day transactions. Web wallets, accessed through web browsers, offer quick access to cryptocurrencies but come with higher security risks due to storing private keys online.

To set up a cryptocurrency wallet, start by researching different wallets and choosing one that aligns with your needs, security preferences, and the cryptocurrencies you intend to store. After downloading or purchasing the wallet, follow the installation instructions and create a strong password and backup phrase. The backup phrase, consisting of random words, is crucial for recovering your wallet in case of loss, theft, or device failure, so make sure to store it securely offline. With your wallet set up, you will receive a public address for each supported cryptocurrency to receive funds and an interface to send cryptocurrencies to other wallets.

Your cryptocurrency wallet's security is of the utmost significance. Regularly back up your wallet's private keys or backup phrase and store them in a safe and offline location. Activate two-factor authentication (2FA) whenever possible to add an extra layer of security. To guarantee you get the most recent security patches, keep your software updated. Beware of phishing attempts and only provide sensitive information to trusted sources. If you plan to store significant quantities of cryptocurrency, think about adopting a hardware wallet, which offers the best level of security by storing your private keys offline.

Properly managing your digital assets is essential for a smooth and secure experience. Diversify your holdings across different wallets and platforms to reduce risk. Keep up with the most recent security risks and advancements in the world of cryptocurrencies. Regularly review your cryptocurrency holdings and consider rebalancing them based on market conditions and your investment goals. Avoid sharing sensitive information about your wallet or holdings with anyone and be cautious when using third-party services that require access to your wallet or private keys.

In conclusion, setting up a cryptocurrency wallet is fundamental for anyone interested in holding, sending, and receiving digital assets. Understanding the different types of wallets, the steps involved in setting up a wallet, and the importance of security measures can empower users to manage their cryptocurrencies confidently.

Following the recommended security measures and best practices, users can safeguard their digital assets and enjoy a secure and seamless cryptocurrency experience. Remember, the responsibility of managing your digital assets rests with you, and exercising caution and diligence can go a long way in protecting your investments and financial future.

Securing Your Cryptocurrency

Cryptocurrencies have revolutionized the financial landscape, offering unprecedented opportunities for financial sovereignty and wealth accumulation. However, the decentralized nature of cryptocurrencies also exposes them to various security risks. The security of your cryptocurrency has become a top priority for users and investors as interest in digital assets continues to surge. This section will explore the critical aspects of securing your cryptocurrency, including safeguarding private keys, using secure wallets, implementing best security practices, recognizing common threats, and staying vigilant against potential risks. By understanding and implementing these essential security measures, users can confidently protect their digital assets in cryptocurrencies' dynamic and rapidly evolving world.

At the core of cryptocurrency security lies the concept of private keys. Private keys are cryptographic keys that grant access to digital assets and allow you to sign transactions on the blockchain. It is essential to always keep your private keys secure and confidential. Avoid storing them on internet-connected devices or cloud services, as these are susceptible to hacking attempts. Instead, consider using hardware or paper wallets to keep your private keys offline and avoid potential cyber threats.

Selecting the right wallet is crucial for safeguarding your cryptocurrency. Several types of wallets are available, each with varying levels of security. Hardware wallets are tangible objects that hold private keys offline. Because they are not linked to the internet while not in use, they provide a high level of security. Popular hardware wallets include Ledger, Trezor, and KeepKey. On the other hand, software wallets come in different varieties such as desktop wallets, mobile wallets, and web wallets. Desktop wallets are software applications installed on computers, offering full control over your private keys. Mobile wallets, designed for smartphones and tablets, provide portability and convenience for day-to-day transactions. Web wallets, accessed through web browsers, offer quick access to cryptocurrencies but come with higher security risks due to storing private keys online.

In addition to choosing secure wallets, implementing best security practices is essential for protecting your cryptocurrency. Activating two-factor authentication (2FA) adds a further layer of security to your accounts, demanding an additional verification step, typically a one-time code sent to your mobile device, when logging in or conducting certain actions. Create strong and unique passwords for all your cryptocurrency-related accounts, wallets, and exchanges. Avoid reusing passwords and consider using a password manager to securely track complex passwords. Update your operating system and wallet software frequently to make sure you have the most recent security updates. Regularly backup your wallet's private keys or recovery phrases and store them securely offline. In case of loss, damage, or theft, this backup will be essential for restoring your wallet.

Understanding common security threats is crucial for proactive protection against potential risks. Be cautious of phishing emails or websites that attempt to deceive you into revealing your login credentials or private keys. Always verify the website's or email's authenticity before providing any sensitive information. Malicious software and keyloggers can record your keystrokes and compromise your passwords or private keys. Use reputable antivirus software and avoid downloading files from untrusted sources. Be wary of social engineering attacks where scammers manipulate individuals into divulging sensitive information. Avoid sharing private keys, recovery phrases, or personal details with unknown or unverified individuals. Only use wallets and exchanges from reputable sources. Scammers may create fake websites or apps to steal your cryptocurrency, so double-check URLs and read reviews before using new services.

Maintaining vigilance is essential in the dynamic world of cryptocurrencies. Maintain up-to-date knowledge on the newest security risks, industry best practices, and advancements. Following reputable cryptocurrency news sources and forums can provide valuable insights. Regularly review your wallet and exchange accounts for any suspicious activity. Report any unauthorized transactions or anomalies to the platform's customer support immediately. Share your knowledge about cryptocurrency security with friends and family to help them protect their digital assets as well.

CHAPTER VI

Understanding
Cryptocurrency Mining

What is Mining?

Mining is an integral and fascinating aspect of the cryptocurrency ecosystem. It is the process by which new transactions are added to the blockchain and new coins are minted. Mining plays a pivotal role in securing the network, validating transactions, and ensuring the decentralization and immutability of blockchain-based cryptocurrencies. In this section, we will explore the concept of mining in cryptocurrency, its significance, the mining process, the role of miners, and the challenges it presents. Understanding mining will provide valuable insights into the underlying technology that drives cryptocurrencies and facilitates peer-to-peer transactions securely and transparently.

The act of validating as well as adding new transactions to the blockchain is known as mining in the context of cryptocurrencies. It is a crucial component of the Proof of Work (PoW) consensus mechanism employed by many cryptocurrencies, including Bitcoin, Ethereum, and Litecoin. The primary objectives of mining are to achieve network security, prevent double-spending, and create new coins or tokens as a reward for miners' efforts.

In the mining process, computational power is used to solve challenging mathematical puzzles. These puzzles, known as cryptographic hashes, are challenging to solve but easy to verify. Miners compete to find the correct nonce (a random number) that, when combined with the data of the new block and the previous block's hash, generates a hash that meets specific criteria, often defined by the difficulty level set by the network. The first miner to discover the right nonce can produce a new block that is added to the blockchain and receives the mining reward.

Miners are crucial participants in the cryptocurrency network. They ensure the validity of transactions and maintain the integrity of the blockchain by reaching a consensus on the order of transactions. The process of mining requires substantial computational power and energy resources. Miners compete against each other, and the process is resource-intensive, making it difficult for any single entity to control most of the network and compromise its security.

Miners are rewarded for their efforts and computational power with newly created coins or tokens and any transaction fees users pay. The mining reward incentivizes miners to dedicate their resources to secure and maintain the network. In Bitcoin, for instance, the mining reward is halved approximately every four years through a process known as "halving." This mechanism controls the inflation rate and ultimately cap the total bitcoin supply at 21 million.

The energy-intensive nature of mining has raised concerns about its environmental impact. The huge computational power needed for mining, according to critics, results in significant energy use and carbon emissions. Addressing these environmental issues and investigating more sustainable consensus techniques, including Proof of Stake (PoS), have grown in importance as the use of cryptocurrencies increases.

The increasing concentration of mining power in some cryptocurrencies has sparked debates about the centralization of mining. As mining becomes more competitive and resource-intensive, large mining farms with substantial computational power have emerged. This concentration of power raises concerns about the potential for a single entity to gain control over the network, leading to centralization and potential security risks.

While Proof of Work remains the dominant consensus mechanism for many cryptocurrencies, other alternatives, such as Proof of Stake as well as Delegated Proof of Stake (DPoS), have gained popularity. These alternative consensus mechanisms offer potential solutions to the energy consumption and centralization concerns associated with Proof of Work.

As the cryptocurrency ecosystem evolves, mining is likely to undergo significant changes. Developers and researchers are exploring novel consensus mechanisms that offer increased scalability, security, and sustainability. With the rising interest in blockchain technology and decentralized applications, the role of mining in securing and maintaining the integrity of blockchain networks will remain a fundamental aspect of the cryptocurrency revolution.

Proof-of-Work vs. Proof-of-Stake

By offering decentralized and secure methods for peer-to-peer transactions, blockchain technology has transformed numerous sectors. At the heart of these blockchain networks lie consensus mechanisms, which ensure agreement among participants on the validity of transactions and the ledger's state. Two prominent consensus mechanisms are Proof-of-Work (PoW) and Proof-of-Stake (PoS). In this section, we will delve into the concepts of PoW and PoS, compare their strengths and weaknesses, and explore their impact on blockchain networks' security, energy consumption, scalability, and decentralization. Understanding the differences between PoW and PoS will provide valuable insights into the future of blockchain development and the quest for more efficient, sustainable, and secure consensus mechanisms.

Proof-of-Work is the original consensus mechanism introduced by Satoshi Nakamoto with the creation of Bitcoin. In the PoW mechanism, miners compete to solve complex mathematical puzzles using computational power. The first miner to solve a block of transactions can add it to the blockchain, and they are rewarded with newly minted coins or tokens along with transaction fees. PoW makes it more difficult for malicious actors to change the blockchain's history or engage in double-spending by guaranteeing that a significant portion of the network's computational power is controlled by honest participants.

One of the strengths of Proof-of-Work is its security. PoW is highly secure due to the computational power required to control the network. To change the blockchain, an attacker has to have over 50% of the network's computing power (a 51% attack), which gets harder as the network grows bigger. Additionally, PoW encourages decentralization, as anyone with sufficient computational power can participate as a miner, reducing the risk of centralization and single points of failure. Furthermore, PoW has a proven track record, having been in use since the inception of Bitcoin and demonstrating its robustness and resilience against attacks for over a decade.

However, Proof-of-Work has its challenges. One major concern is its energy consumption. PoW is energy-intensive, requiring vast amounts of computational power to solve puzzles. This has led to concerns about cryptocurrencies' environmental impact and carbon footprint using PoW. Moreover, as the number of transactions and users on the network increases, PoW can become slower and less scalable due to the time it takes to validate and add blocks to the blockchain.

Proof-of-Stake, on the other hand, is an alternative consensus mechanism that seeks to overcome PoW's energy consumption and scalability issues. In a proof-of-stake (PoS) system, validators, sometimes referred to as "stakers," are selected to build new blocks based on the quantity of coins they own and are willing to "stake" or lock up as collateral. A validator is chosen to construct a block more frequently when the stakes are larger. PoS eliminates the need for competitive mining and reduces the energy consumption associated with PoW.

One of the strengths of Proof-of-Stake is its energy efficiency. PoS requires significantly less energy than PoW since it does not involve resource-intensive computational puzzles. Rather than choosing validators through mining, new blocks are created by validators based on their stakes. PoS is also more scalable since block creation is based on the number of coins validators hold, not computational power. This allows PoS-based blockchains to process transactions more quickly and efficiently as the network grows. Moreover, PoS has a lower carbon footprint than PoW, making it a more environmentally friendly consensus mechanism.

However, Proof-of-Stake also has its weaknesses. Critics argue that PoS could lead to centralization as those with a significant stake could have more influence and control over the network. This could create a wealth-based hierarchy, undermining the decentralized ethos of blockchain technology. Additionally, long-term security concerns arise if the value of the staked coins is significantly lower than the potential gains from malicious behavior, which may incentivize dishonest behavior by validators.

Some blockchain projects have adopted hybrid approaches, combining PoW and PoS elements to leverage each mechanism's strengths. For example, in the PoW/PoS hybrid model, PoW is used for block creation, while PoS is utilized for block validation and consensus. This combination aims to balance security, decentralization, and scalability while reducing energy consumption.

Bitcoin and many other well-established cryptocurrencies like Ethereum and Litecoin predominantly use PoW. On the other hand,

PoS has gained popularity and is implemented by cryptocurrencies like Ethereum 2.0, Cardano, and Tezos.

As blockchain technology evolves, the quest for more efficient, sustainable, and secure consensus mechanisms remains ongoing. Research and development efforts are exploring new consensus models, such as Proof-of-Authority, Delegated Proof-of-Stake, and Byzantine Fault Tolerance. These models aim to address the limitations of existing mechanisms and provide better solutions for blockchain scalability, security, and decentralization.

Mining Challenges and Environmental Concerns

Mining, the process by which new transactions are added to the blockchain and new coins are minted, is a fundamental aspect of many cryptocurrencies' operations. While mining has been instrumental in establishing blockchain networks' decentralized and secure nature, it also comes with significant challenges and environmental concerns. In this section, we will explore the various challenges miners face, the environmental impact of mining activities, and the efforts being made to address these concerns. Understanding the complexities of mining challenges and environmental considerations is crucial for developing sustainable and responsible blockchain solutions that align with the global quest for a greener and more eco-friendly future.

Mining in cryptocurrencies involves solving complex mathematical puzzles using computational power. This process is resource-intensive and highly competitive. As blockchain networks grow in popularity, the mining difficulty increases, necessitating even greater computational power to secure the network and validate transactions. The challenges faced by miners include rising energy costs, hardware costs, and the potential for centralization. Rising energy costs result from the ever-increasing complexity of mining puzzles, demanding substantial computational power, which leads to higher energy consumption and operational costs for miners. Additionally, miners need specialized hardware, such as Application-Specific Integrated Circuits (ASICs) or Graphics Processing Units (GPUs), to compete effectively in the mining race. These hardware components can be expensive, making it challenging for small-scale miners to participate profitably. Moreover, as mining becomes more competitive and resource-intensive, larger mining farms and pools with significant computational power have emerged, leading to concerns about centralization and the potential concentration of mining power.

The energy-intensive nature of mining has raised substantial environmental concerns. The colossal computational power required to solve mining puzzles consumes vast amounts of electricity, contributing to significant carbon emissions and a high carbon footprint. The key environmental concerns of mining are carbon emissions, electronic waste, and ecological impact. The energy-intensive mining process relies heavily on fossil fuels, resulting in significant carbon emissions. As the mining industry expands, these emissions contribute to global carbon dioxide levels, exacerbating climate change. Additionally, the constant need for upgrading and replacing mining hardware generates electronic waste, often resulting in landfills and threatening the environment and human health. Moreover, in some regions, mining operations have led to the exploitation of natural resources, including deforestation and habitat destruction, causing adverse effects on local ecosystems and biodiversity.

The mining industry and blockchain community recognize the importance of addressing the challenges and environmental impact of mining. Several initiatives and approaches are being explored to mitigate these concerns. One such approach is increasing energy efficiency and transitioning to renewable energy sources. By employing renewable energy sources like solar, wind, and hydroelectric power, which can considerably reduce carbon emissions, efforts are being undertaken to lessen the environmental impact of mining operations. Additionally, researchers are developing more energy-efficient mining hardware to minimize electricity consumption and waste heat generation. This includes exploring alternative hardware designs and materials that can enhance the efficiency of mining processes.

Moreover, some blockchain projects are exploring alternatives to the traditional Proof-of-Work (PoW) consensus mechanism, such as Proof-of-Stake (PoS). Instead of using competitive mining, PoS uses validators who are selected to build new blocks based on the amount of coins they "stake" or lock up as collateral. PoS is a more environmentally friendly alternative to PoW because it does not require energy-intensive mining activities. Another initiative to address environmental concerns is investing in carbon offsetting and sustainability projects. To offset their carbon impact, several mining operations are funding initiatives that lower greenhouse gas emissions, such reforestation and renewable energy projects.

Engaging with local communities and adhering to environmental regulations is essential for responsible mining practices. Collaborating with stakeholders can foster transparency and sustainability, ensuring that mining activities have a minimal negative impact on local environments and communities. Responsible mining practices require continuous efforts from all stakeholders involved in the blockchain industry.

As blockchain technology evolves, the industry must adopt more eco-friendly and sustainable practices. Embracing energy-efficient consensus mechanisms, exploring renewable energy sources, optimizing mining hardware, and engaging in carbon offsetting initiatives are all steps towards a greener mining industry. Blockchain innovators and users play a critical role in shaping the future of technology. Blockchain projects can demonstrate a commitment to responsible practices by prioritizing sustainability and seeking energy-efficient solutions. Additionally, users can support eco-friendly projects and platforms that employ greener mining approaches.

CHAPTER VII

The Mechanics of Cryptocurrency Transactions

Public and Private Keys

In the world of digital communication and transactions, security and privacy are of paramount importance. Public and private keys are cryptographic tools that play a central role in securing data, authenticating users, and enabling secure communication in various applications, including cryptocurrencies, secure messaging, and online banking. In this section, we will delve into the concepts of public and private keys, their role in asymmetric encryption, how they facilitate secure digital communication, and their significance in blockchain technology and cryptocurrencies. Understanding public and private keys is crucial for grasping the underlying principles of cryptographic security and appreciating the robustness of modern digital systems.

The public and private keys are two separate but mathematically connected keys used in asymmetric encryption, sometimes referred to as public-key cryptography. The idea behind asymmetric encryption addresses the challenges posed by traditional symmetric encryption, where a single shared key must be exchanged between parties for secure communication. Asymmetric encryption overcomes this limitation by using a pair of keys, providing enhanced security and privacy.

As the name suggests, the public key is publicly available and used for encryption. It is generated by an algorithm that derives it from the corresponding private key. Anyone can access and use the public key to encrypt messages or data for a specific recipient. However, it is computationally infeasible to reverse-engineer the private key from the public key, ensuring the security of the encryption process.

The private key is the counterpart to the public key and is generated simultaneously with it. It must be kept secret and known only to the owner. The private key is used for decryption, and it allows the recipient to decrypt messages or data that have been encrypted using their corresponding public key. The security of the entire asymmetric encryption system hinges on the secrecy and protection of private keys.

Utilizing both private and public keys to encrypt and decrypt messages is a simple process. For instance, Alice uses Bob's public key to encrypt a message that she wants to send to Bob securely, making sure that only Bob's private key is able to decrypt it. Conversely, when Bob receives the encrypted message, he uses his private key to decrypt it and read the original message. This process guarantees that only the intended recipient can access the message's contents, providing a robust and secure means of communication.

Public and private keys also facilitate the creation of digital signatures. With the help of a digital signature, a sender can demonstrate the reliability and validity of a message or document. To generate a digital signature, the sender uses their private key to encrypt a hash value of the message. The resulting encrypted hash, known as the digital signature, is appended to the message. The digital signature may be decrypted and the hash value can be obtained by the recipient using the sender's public key after they get the message. By comparing the decrypted hash to a newly computed hash of the received message, the recipient can verify the message's integrity and authenticate the sender.

The utilization of public and private keys is fundamental to blockchain technology and cryptocurrencies. In blockchain networks, users use unique public and private key pairs to conduct secure and transparent transactions. A user must generate a transaction that contains the recipient's public key in order to transmit cryptocurrency to another user. The transaction is then signed using the sender's private key, building a digital signature that verifies the transaction's authenticity and ensures that only the sender can authorize the transfer.

Securing public and private keys is crucial to maintaining the integrity and confidentiality of digital communication and transactions. In order to prevent unwanted access to their sensitive information, users must preserve their private keys securely and refrain from disclosing them with anyone. There are various methods of key storage, ranging from hardware wallets and secure software solutions to multi-factor authentication systems. Additionally, users should regularly update and back up their key pairs to safeguard against potential loss or theft.

As the digital landscape evolves, public and private keys will remain essential components of cryptographic security. Asymmetric encryption and digital signatures have already found applications in various domains, including secure messaging, e-commerce, and identity verification. With the rise of blockchain technology, public and private keys will play an even more significant role in facilitating secure and decentralized peer-to-peer transactions and data management.

The Role of Miners and Nodes

In blockchain technology, miners and nodes are essential components that form the backbone of decentralized networks. Miners are responsible for validating transactions, securing the network, and creating new blocks, while nodes are the distributed infrastructure that maintains and propagates the blockchain's data. Together, miners and nodes play a crucial role in ensuring blockchain systems' transparency, security, and efficiency.

Miners are integral to the operation of proof-of-work (PoW) based blockchains, such as Bitcoin. Their primary function is to validate and confirm transactions within the network, ensuring that only legitimate transactions are included in the blockchain. Mining includes employing computational power to solve challenging mathematical puzzles. New coins as well as transaction fees are awarded to the first miner that solves the puzzle and adds a block of confirmed transactions to the blockchain. Miners undertake several tasks: transaction validation, block creation, consensus maintenance, and block rewards.

On the other hand, nodes are the distributed network participants that store and propagate the blockchain's data. Each node in the network maintains a complete copy of the blockchain ledger, making it decentralized and resilient to single points of failure. Nodes contribute to the robustness and security of blockchain networks through data propagation, consensus verification, network stability, and the distinction between full nodes and light nodes.

Consensus mechanisms like PoW and PoS depend on the collaboration of miners and nodes to maintain the integrity of the blockchain. In PoW, miners compete to solve computational puzzles, while nodes verify the blocks mined by miners, ensuring the network's consistency and security. In PoS, nodes perform similar functions, but validators are chosen based on staked coins rather than computational power.

The synergy between miners and nodes ensures a decentralized, trustless network where transparent and immutable transactions are. Miners create new blocks and validate transactions, while nodes store and propagate the blockchain's data, verify transactions, and maintain consensus. This collaborative effort ensures blockchain systems' security, transparency, and efficiency.

However, scalability remains a challenge for blockchain networks. As the number of transactions and users increases, the system must handle higher transaction volumes without sacrificing security or decentralization. Scalability is affected by block size, block time, and the consensus mechanism employed. For example, in PoW, the time to mine a block affects the overall transaction throughput, leading to slower processing during peak times.

As blockchain technology evolves, miners and nodes will play a pivotal role in enabling trustless and decentralized peer-to-peer transactions, contributing to the vision of a more inclusive and decentralized digital future. The role of miners and nodes in blockchain technology will continue to evolve with the advancement of the industry. As consensus mechanisms evolve beyond PoW and PoS, miners and nodes may have different roles and responsibilities in ensuring network security and efficiency. Additionally, advancements in hardware and software technologies may lead to more energy-efficient mining and enhanced node capabilities.

Confirmations and Transaction Speeds

In blockchain technology, confirmations and transaction speeds are critical factors that dictate the efficiency and security of digital transactions. Blockchain networks, which are decentralized and trustless systems, depend on a consensus method to verify and store block transactions. However, the trade-off between transaction speed and the number of confirmations required for transaction finality poses significant challenges.

The amount of blocks that have been added to the blockchain following a certain transaction is referred to as confirmations. Each additional block added to the blockchain serves as a confirmation level, further validating the transaction's inclusion in the network.

The more confirmations a transaction has, the more secure and immutable it becomes. Confirmations are fundamental to blockchain security as they prevent double-spending and ensure the ledger's integrity.

Transaction speed, however, refers to the time it takes for a transaction to be processed and added to the blockchain. In traditional financial systems, transactions can be processed quickly, often in seconds. However, in blockchain networks, transaction speed is influenced by several factors, including the consensus mechanism, network congestion, and block size.

There is an inherent trade-off between the number of confirmations required for transaction finality and transaction speeds. The more confirmations a transaction requires, the longer it takes for the transaction to be considered fully validated and secure. On the other hand, reducing the number of confirmations needed can increase transaction speeds but may compromise the security and immutability of the transaction. Striking the right balance between the two is a crucial challenge for blockchain developers and users.

Different consensus mechanisms have varying effects on transaction speeds. Proof-of-Work (PoW) based blockchains, like Bitcoin, typically have longer block times due to the energy-intensive mining process required to add new blocks. This results in slower transaction speeds and a higher number of required confirmations for transaction finality. On the other hand, Proof-of-Stake (PoS) based blockchains can have faster block times and lower transaction fees, allowing quicker transaction speeds and a reduced number of required confirmations.

Blockchain developers and researchers have been actively exploring solutions to optimize transaction speeds without compromising security. Layer 2 solutions, such as the Raiden Network for Ethereum and the Lightning Network for Bitcoin, aim to increase transaction speeds by conducting transactions off-chain and settling them later on the main blockchain. These solutions enable faster and cheaper micro-transactions while maintaining the security of the main blockchain.

Another method is sharding, which separates the blockchain network into more manageable, more compact portions known as shards. Each shard processes its transactions independently, allowing for parallel processing and increased transaction speeds. Sharding is being explored by various blockchain projects to improve scalability and reduce confirmation times.

As blockchain technology continues to evolve, advancements in consensus mechanisms, scaling solutions, and network upgrades will likely lead to faster transaction speeds and more efficient confirmations. The ongoing research and development in the blockchain space aim to address these challenges and optimize the performance of blockchain networks.

CHAPTER VIII

The Economics of Cryptocurrencies

Supply and Demand Dynamics

Cryptocurrencies have emerged as a disruptive force in finance, introducing a new paradigm of decentralized digital assets. The economics of cryptocurrencies are intricately linked to the principles of supply and demand, which govern the valuation, price volatility, and overall market dynamics of these digital assets.

Supply and demand are fundamental economic principles that underpin market dynamics across various asset classes, including cryptocurrencies. Supply refers to the quantity of a particular asset available in the market, while demand denotes the desire and willingness of buyers to acquire that asset at a given price. The equilibrium price at which the asset is traded is determined by the relationship between supply and demand.

Many cryptocurrencies, including Bitcoin, have a capped supply, meaning a finite number of coins will ever be created. For instance, there are only 21 million Bitcoins available overall. This scarcity is a crucial factor in Bitcoin's value proposition, as it positions the cryptocurrency as a digital store of value akin to precious metals like gold. The fixed supply of Bitcoin also influences its demand, with investors seeking to acquire the asset as a hedge against traditional fiat currencies' inflationary tendencies.

In some cryptocurrencies, new coins are created through mining or coin issuance to reward network participants who contribute computing power or stake their coins in the network. The rate of coin issuance can impact the overall supply and, consequently, the market value of the cryptocurrency. Cryptocurrencies with high inflation rates may face downward price pressure, as an abundance of new coins entering the market can dilute the value of existing holdings.

A multitude of factors can influence the demand for cryptocurrencies. Some of the key demand drivers include speculation and investment, practical use cases and adoption in various industries, financial uncertainty, and the regulatory environment. Cryptocurrencies often attract speculative interest from investors seeking to capitalize on price volatility and potential future gains. The perception of cryptocurrencies as alternative investments or speculative assets contributes to their demand.

The demand for cryptocurrencies is also influenced by their practical use cases and adoption in various industries. Cryptocurrencies that enable efficient cross-border payments, decentralized finance (DeFi) applications, or smart contracts garner significant demand from users and enterprises. In times of economic uncertainty or political instability, cryptocurrencies can serve as a hedge against traditional financial systems and fiat currencies. The demand for cryptocurrencies may rise during periods of economic turbulence.

Demand for cryptocurrencies is significantly influenced by the regulatory environment. Favorable regulations and institutional acceptance can boost demand, while unfavorable rules can lead to reduced interest and demand. Furthermore, the ease of buying and selling cryptocurrencies is influenced by the liquidity situation, which affects price stability. Exchanges also offer trading pairs facilitating conversions between cryptocurrencies and fiat currencies, further impacting demand and price dynamics.

In the cryptocurrency market, the interaction of supply and demand can cause significant price volatility. Sudden shifts in market sentiment, news events, or regulatory developments can trigger sharp price movements. Due to the relatively nascent and unregulated nature of the cryptocurrency market, it is more susceptible to speculation and price manipulation, leading to extreme price swings.

Cryptocurrencies with fixed supply, such as Bitcoin, experience supply shocks due to events like the halving. Bitcoin's block reward halves approximately every four years, reducing the rate of new coin issuance. An imbalance between supply and demand could develop from this halving occurrence, which historically has led to price increases.

As the cryptocurrency ecosystem matures, efforts to enhance scalability, reduce transaction costs, and address regulatory uncertainties will likely shape the future of cryptocurrencies' supply and demand dynamics. Institutional adoption, technological advancements, and increased mainstream acceptance could further drive demand and cement cryptocurrencies' position in the global financial landscape.

Price Volatility and Market Factors

Cryptocurrencies have captivated the financial world with their meteoric rise, but their price volatility remains a defining characteristic. Unlike traditional assets, cryptocurrency prices can experience extreme fluctuations within short time frames. Price volatility is the degree of change in an asset's price over a given time period. In the context of cryptocurrencies, price volatility is common, with prices sometimes experiencing substantial swings in hours or even minutes. This volatility stands in stark contrast to more established financial instruments like stocks or commodities, which typically exhibit lower degrees of price fluctuation.

A myriad of factors contribute to the price volatility in the cryptocurrency market. Some of the key drivers include speculation and sentiment, market liquidity, regulatory developments, technological upgrades and forks, market news and events, market manipulation, and external market factors. Cryptocurrencies are often subject to speculative trading, where investors make short-term bets on price movements. Fueled by news, social media, and rumors, market sentiment can drive rapid price swings, amplifying volatility. Cryptocurrencies with lower trading volumes are more susceptible to price manipulation and sharp price movements. Illiquid markets lack the depth to absorb large buy or sell orders, leading to exaggerated price changes.

Government regulations or announcements regarding cryptocurrency usage and trading can significantly impact prices. Favorable laws may drive positive price trends, while adverse regulatory news can lead to sharp declines. Technological upgrades or contentious forks can cause uncertainty in the community, leading to diverging opinions and price volatility. Forks, where a cryptocurrency splits into two separate assets, can create confusion and fluctuations in value. News related to security breaches, exchange hacks, partnerships, or major developments can trigger significant price movements as traders react to new information.

Market sentiment plays a vital role in driving price volatility in the cryptocurrency market. The behavior of market participants, fueled by fear, greed, or FOMO (fear of missing out), can trigger cascading effects on prices. Positive news or announcements can cause a surge in demand, leading to a price rally, while negative sentiment can trigger panic selling, resulting in sharp declines. Social media and online communities also play a significant role in shaping market sentiment. Influential figures, celebrities, or prominent industry players expressing their opinions on social media platforms can lead to rapid shifts in sentiment and subsequent price movements.

The price volatility of cryptocurrencies has several implications for investors, adoption, and the broader financial landscape. It presents both risks and opportunities for investors. While it can lead to substantial profits for astute traders, it also exposes them to significant losses if they fail to anticipate market movements correctly. Price volatility can hinder the mainstream adoption of cryptocurrencies for everyday transactions. The unpredictability of prices makes it challenging for merchants and consumers to rely on cryptocurrencies for stable pricing and consistent value. The extreme price volatility and potential for market manipulation have drawn regulatory attention. Governments and financial watchdogs closely monitor the cryptocurrency market to protect investors and maintain market integrity.

Various strategies are employed to mitigate the impact of price volatility in the cryptocurrency market. Diversifying a cryptocurrency portfolio across different assets can reduce the risk of exposure to the price movements of individual cryptocurrencies. Stablecoins provide a mechanism to maintain value during times of extreme volatility since they are anchored to fiat currencies or other stable assets. Investors use risk management techniques, such as stop-loss orders and hedging strategies, to limit potential losses during sharp price declines. A long-term investment approach can help investors weather short-term price fluctuations and focus on the potential of underlying technologies and use cases.

As the cryptocurrency market matures, price volatility will likely gradually subside. Increased institutional participation, regulatory clarity, and market infrastructure developments may contribute to a more stable and liquid market environment. Additionally, price volatility may normalize as adoption increases and cryptocurrencies find broader real-world use cases. As the ecosystem continues to evolve and stakeholders navigate the dynamic nature of cryptocurrency prices, the potential of blockchain technology and decentralized digital assets remains a compelling force in the global financial landscape.

Factors Affecting Cryptocurrency Prices

Cryptocurrencies have become a significant player in the financial landscape, attracting attention from investors, institutions, and the public. One of the most intriguing aspects of cryptocurrencies is their price movements, which can be highly volatile and subject to rapid changes. Investors and market participants must have a thorough understanding of the variables affecting cryptocurrency pricing in order to make informed decisions.

Market sentiment and speculative activity both have a significant impact on cryptocurrency pricing. The behavior of investors, driven by emotions such as fear, greed, and FOMO (fear of missing out), plays a significant role in driving price movements. Positive news, partnerships, or endorsements from influential figures can create a sense of optimism and drive demand, leading to price rallies. Conversely, negative news, security breaches, or regulatory uncertainties can trigger panic selling and sharp price declines. Speculative trading, where investors make short-term bets on price movements, can amplify volatility and contribute to short-term price swings.

Supply and demand are critical in determining cryptocurrency prices, as with any asset. Cryptocurrencies with limited or capped supplies, like Bitcoin, are often perceived as more valuable due to their scarcity. The fixed supply of some cryptocurrencies creates a sense of digital scarcity, akin to precious metals like gold. On the other hand, the demand for cryptocurrencies is influenced by factors such as their practical use cases, adoption in various industries, and investor sentiment. When demand outpaces supply, prices rise, and vice versa.

The underlying technology of cryptocurrencies is a crucial determinant of their value. Technological developments and upgrades can have a significant impact on cryptocurrency prices. For instance, upgrades that enhance scalability, security, and transaction speeds can increase confidence in the cryptocurrency's future potential, leading to higher demand and prices. Additionally, new features, functionalities, or use cases can attract more users and investors to a cryptocurrency, influencing its price.

The regulatory environment is a critical factor influencing cryptocurrency prices. Government regulations, announcements, and legal developments can create uncertainty and affect market sentiment. Favorable rules that provide clarity and legitimacy to cryptocurrencies can increase adoption and demand, driving higher prices. Conversely, stringent or restrictive regulations can dampen investor enthusiasm and negatively impact prices. The lack of uniform regulatory frameworks across different countries adds to the complexity of the cryptocurrency market.

Market liquidity, characterized by the ease of buying and selling assets without significantly affecting their prices, is vital for stable cryptocurrency prices. Cryptocurrencies with higher trading volumes and deeper liquidity are less susceptible to price manipulation and extreme price swings. On the other hand, illiquid markets are more prone to sharp price movements, as a large buy or sell order can disproportionately impact prices.

Broader macroeconomic trends and events can also influence cryptocurrency prices. For example, economic crises, inflationary pressures, or geopolitical uncertainties may drive investors towards cryptocurrencies as a hedge against traditional financial systems. Similarly, changes in interest rates, global economic growth, and fiscal policies can impact investor sentiment and capital flows into the cryptocurrency market.

Media coverage and public perception can shape cryptocurrency prices. Positive media coverage, endorsements from prominent figures, and increased public awareness can contribute to price rallies. Conversely, negative media attention or sensationalized stories can lead to fear-driven sell-offs and price declines. The impact of media on cryptocurrency prices highlights the importance of information dissemination and its effect on market sentiment.

Cryptocurrency prices can also be influenced by their integration with traditional finance and the global financial system. Partnerships with conventional financial institutions, support from established players, and inclusion on regulated trading platforms can boost confidence in cryptocurrencies and attract more institutional investment, leading to price appreciation.

The relative lack of regulation in cryptocurrency makes it susceptible to market manipulation. Pump-and-dump schemes, where specific individuals or groups artificially inflate prices before selling off, are common occurrences. Such schemes can lead to significant price spikes followed by steep declines, causing losses for unsuspecting investors.

Technological vulnerabilities and security risks can also impact cryptocurrency prices. Hacks, cyberattacks, or vulnerabilities in the underlying blockchain technology can lead to loss of funds and erode investor confidence, resulting in price declines.

CHAPTER IX

Legal and Regulatory Landscape

Government Regulations and Bans

The rapid rise of cryptocurrencies has sparked interest and concern among governments worldwide. As digital assets gain prominence, the need for regulatory oversight and policymaking has become evident. Governments face the challenge of balancing embracing innovation and protecting investors, consumers, and financial systems. In this section, we will explore the complexities of government regulations and bans on cryptocurrencies, examining the varied approaches taken by different countries, the potential impact on the cryptocurrency market, and the implications for the future of this transformative asset class.

Governments around the world have adopted diverse approaches to regulating cryptocurrencies. Some countries have embraced digital assets by implementing comprehensive regulatory frameworks that provide clarity, protect consumers, and prevent illicit activities. These regulatory regimes often require cryptocurrency exchanges to comply with Know Your Customer (KYC) as well as Anti-Money Laundering (AML) regulations. Additionally, some countries have established licensing requirements for cryptocurrency service providers and seek to ensure the financial system's stability.

In contrast, other countries have taken a more cautious or restrictive stance, treating cryptocurrencies as speculative assets or outright banning them. Concerns over investor protection, money laundering, tax evasion, and potential threats to financial stability have prompted some governments to issue bans or impose stringent restrictions on cryptocurrency activities.

Government regulations and bans can have a profound impact on the cryptocurrency market. Positive and supportive regulatory environments can foster investor confidence, increasing adoption and market growth. Institutional investors that have been reluctant to enter the market because of uncertainty around legal and compliance requirements may be drawn in by regulatory clarity.

On the other hand, restrictive regulations or outright bans can stifle innovation and drive cryptocurrency-related businesses to operate in more crypto-friendly jurisdictions. In some cases, regulatory uncertainty and fear of potential prohibitions may lead to market downturns and increased price volatility. This uncertainty may discourage widespread adoption and obstruct the incorporation of cryptocurrencies into the established financial system.

One of the primary motivations behind government regulations is to protect consumers and investors. The cryptocurrency market is still relatively nascent and lacks the same level of investor protection as traditional financial markets. Scams, fraudulent schemes, and hacking incidents have highlighted the need for regulatory oversight to safeguard individuals from financial losses and unscrupulous actors.

Regulatory frameworks that enforce transparency, security standards, and consumer education can enhance investor safety. Cryptocurrency exchanges that are authorized and governed are more likely to have strong security measures in place and follow best practices, which lowers the likelihood of theft and hacking.

The decentralized and pseudonymous character of cryptocurrencies has sparked worries about their potential application in illegal practices like money laundering, terrorism financing, and tax evasion. Governments scrutinize these risks and aim to develop regulations that mitigate such abuses while preserving the benefits of blockchain technology.

Cryptocurrencies' traceability and transparency on public blockchains enable authorities to track suspicious transactions and identify potential criminal activities. Regulatory measures, such as mandatory KYC and AML compliance for cryptocurrency businesses, are crucial in reducing illicit financial flows.

Implementing effective and balanced cryptocurrency regulations presents numerous challenges and opportunities for governments. One significant challenge is the international nature of cryptocurrencies, as they operate across borders without geographical limitations. This characteristic makes it difficult for individual countries to enforce regulations effectively, necessitating international cooperation and harmonization of regulatory approaches.

However, well-crafted regulations can also present opportunities for economic growth and technological innovation. Embracing cryptocurrencies can attract blockchain-based businesses, startups, and talent to a country, fostering a vibrant and innovative ecosystem. Additionally, embracing financial technology (fintech) and blockchain innovation can enhance a country's global competitiveness and position it as a leader in the digital economy.

Finding the right balance in cryptocurrency regulation is crucial. Excessive regulations can stifle innovation and drive businesses to more favorable jurisdictions. On the other hand, insufficient regulations may expose consumers and investors to higher risks and hinder broader market adoption.

Governments face the challenge of continuously adapting regulations to keep pace with the fast-evolving cryptocurrency industry. Flexible and adaptive regulations that promote innovation while safeguarding investors and consumers are essential for fostering a healthy and sustainable cryptocurrency ecosystem.

Given the global nature of cryptocurrencies, coordination and cooperation among countries are vital to address cross-border challenges. International efforts to combat money laundering, terrorist financing, and other illicit activities involving cryptocurrencies require harmonizing regulatory frameworks and information sharing.

Global organizations such as the G20 and the Financial Action Task Force (FATF) have recognized the importance of international cooperation in regulating cryptocurrencies. Collaborative efforts can help develop standardized regulatory guidelines that balance innovation and consumer protection.

The future of cryptocurrency regulations remains uncertain and highly dynamic. As the cryptocurrency market matures and gains wider acceptance, governments are likely to continue refining and updating their regulatory approaches. The development of regulatory sandboxes, which provide a controlled environment for fintech and blockchain startups to test their products, is one-way governments can foster innovation while ensuring compliance with existing laws.

As more countries embrace cryptocurrencies and recognize their potential benefits, others may reconsider their restrictive stances to avoid being left behind in the digital revolution. Ultimately, a collaborative approach that combines global coordination, consumer protection, and balanced regulation is crucial for shaping the future of cryptocurrency regulations.

Tax Implications of Cryptocurrency Transactions

Cryptocurrencies have transformed the financial landscape, offering new opportunities and challenges for investors and governments alike. The tax implications of cryptocurrency transactions must be understood as interest in digital assets grows. In this section, we will explore the various tax considerations related to buying, selling, trading, and using cryptocurrencies, shedding light on the complexities of cryptocurrency taxation and providing guidance on how individuals and businesses can navigate this evolving regulatory landscape.

Determining the tax treatment of cryptocurrencies starts with understanding how they are classified for tax purposes. Cryptocurrencies are regarded as property or assets in many jurisdictions rather than traditional currencies. As such, they may be subject to capital gains tax, similar to stocks or real estate, when bought, sold, or exchanged for goods and services. However, the specific tax treatment can vary significantly depending on the country's tax laws and regulations.

Cryptocurrency transactions give rise to various tax events, and it is essential to be aware of the potential tax liabilities associated with each type of activity. Buying and holding cryptocurrencies does not typically trigger any immediate tax liability. However, any potential capital gains or losses may come into play once the digital assets are sold or exchanged. Capital gains or losses may come from the sale of cryptocurrencies in exchange for fiat money or other digital assets, depending on the difference between the purchase and sale prices. Moreover, using cryptocurrencies to buy goods or services is considered a taxable event in some jurisdictions, as it involves converting the digital asset into its equivalent value in fiat currency for tax purposes. Cryptocurrency mining and staking, where users validate transactions on the blockchain and receive rewards in return, can also have tax implications, as the value of the mined or staked coins at the time of receipt is typically considered taxable income.

Properly reporting cryptocurrency transactions is essential to comply with tax regulations and avoid potential penalties or audits. In some countries, taxpayers may be required to report cryptocurrency holdings and transactions on their tax returns, providing details such as purchase prices, sale prices, and dates of transactions. Additionally, certain countries have specific reporting requirements for large cryptocurrency transactions to prevent tax evasion and illicit activities.

Capital gains and losses play a central role in cryptocurrency taxation. When the value of a cryptocurrency increases from the time of purchase to the time of sale, it results in a capital gain. Conversely, if the value decreases, it leads to a capital loss. Depending on the jurisdiction, these gains and losses may be classified as short-term or long-term, each carrying different tax rates.

The tax implications can be more complex for cryptocurrency traders and investors who frequently engage in buying, selling, and exchanging digital assets. Traders may be subject to different tax rules, such as being classified as self-employed and required to pay self-employment taxes. Moreover, frequent trading can generate a higher volume of taxable events, making accurate record-keeping essential to avoid tax discrepancies.

Cryptocurrency businesses, including exchanges, wallet providers, and other service providers, also have specific tax obligations. They must adhere to corporate tax regulations and, depending on the jurisdiction, may be subject to additional regulatory requirements. Additionally, businesses accepting cryptocurrencies as payment for goods or services must track the value of those transactions for tax reporting purposes.

Cryptocurrency investors and businesses with holdings or transactions in foreign exchanges may be subject to additional reporting requirements. Many countries have implemented measures to monitor overseas financial activities to prevent tax evasion, making it essential for taxpayers to comply with cross-border reporting regulations.

By using the tax loss harvesting approach, investors can minimize their overall tax bill by offsetting capital gains with capital losses. Cryptocurrency investors can utilize this strategy by strategically selling losing positions to offset gains in other investments. However, tax loss harvesting should be done with caution, as certain tax regulations may have specific restrictions on the practice.

The taxation of cryptocurrencies is a rapidly evolving area of tax law. Governments throughout the world are debating the best ways to control and tax these digital assets. As the popularity of cryptocurrencies grows, tax authorities are increasing their focus on enforcing compliance and closing potential loopholes in cryptocurrency taxation. Therefore, it's essential to keep up with the newest regulatory developments to ensure that tax regulations are being followed.

Given the complexity of cryptocurrency taxation and the evolving regulatory landscape, seeking professional advice from tax experts with expertise in cryptocurrency taxation is highly recommended.

Tax professionals can provide guidance on how to navigate the complexities of reporting cryptocurrency transactions, understanding tax liabilities, and optimizing tax strategies.

Compliance and KYC (Know Your Customer)

Cryptocurrencies have revolutionized the financial landscape, offering decentralized and borderless transactions. However, the borderless nature of cryptocurrencies has raised concerns about potential illicit activities, such as money laundering and terrorist financing. Compliance measures, particularly Know Your Customer (KYC), have become essential to address these concerns and foster trust in the cryptocurrency ecosystem.

Compliance and KYC are fundamental elements in cryptocurrency, designed to ensure that businesses and individuals adhere to regulatory standards and prevent illicit activities. KYC processes require cryptocurrency service providers, such as exchanges, wallet providers, and token issuers, to identify and verify the identities of their customers before offering services.

The primary goals of compliance and KYC are twofold: to safeguard the financial system from terrorist financing, money laundering, as well as other financial crimes, and to protect customers from fraud and unauthorized use of their funds.

Cryptocurrencies' decentralized and pseudonymous nature has led some to believe they could be used for illicit purposes. However, blockchain technology's transparent and immutable nature allows authorities to trace and analyze transactions on public blockchains, making it challenging for criminals to launder money or finance terrorist activities entirely undetected.

Compliance and KYC procedures enable cryptocurrency service providers to monitor transactions, identify suspicious activities, and report them to the relevant authorities. Businesses can support the worldwide effort to prevent financial crimes by putting stringent anti-money laundering (AML) measures in place.

Cryptocurrency users often entrust their funds to third-party service providers, such as exchanges, to facilitate trading and transactions. KYC procedures help protect users from fraudulent activities, unauthorized access to their accounts, and potential security breaches.

By verifying customers' identities, service providers can ensure that funds are directed to legitimate recipients and prevent unauthorized access to accounts. Additionally, KYC helps prevent identity theft and impersonation, enhancing user trust and confidence in the cryptocurrency ecosystem.

While compliance and KYC measures are crucial in safeguarding the cryptocurrency ecosystem, they are not without challenges. Some primary challenges include privacy concerns, costs and burden for small businesses, global regulatory fragmentation, and impacts on user experience.

KYC procedures require individuals to provide sensitive personal information, raising concerns about user privacy and data security.

Cryptocurrency users value their privacy, and the collection and storage of personal data can be a source of contention.

Compliance and KYC requirements can be costly and burdensome, particularly for small and emerging cryptocurrency businesses. The expenses associated with compliance may hinder the entry of new players into the market, potentially limiting competition and innovation.

Cryptocurrencies operate across borders, and different countries have varying regulatory frameworks. This global regulatory fragmentation can create challenges for businesses that must navigate other compliance requirements in each jurisdiction they operate.

Lengthy and complex KYC processes can adversely impact user experience. Cumbersome onboarding procedures may discourage potential users, particularly those new to cryptocurrencies, from engaging with cryptocurrency services.

Balancing the need for regulatory compliance with fostering innovation in the cryptocurrency space is a delicate task. While stringent regulations are essential to prevent financial crimes and protect consumers, excessive regulatory burden may stifle innovation and deter businesses from entering the market.

A potential way to strike a balance between compliance and innovation is through the use of regulatory sandboxes, which give fintech companies a regulated environment in which to test their goods and services. Sandboxes allow businesses to experiment with new technologies and services under regulatory supervision, enabling regulators to gain insights while providing businesses with the flexibility to innovate.

Compliance and KYC measures' potential impact on financial inclusion is a key concern. In some regions, most people need access to traditional financial services. Blockchain technologies and cryptocurrencies have the ability to close this gap and provide financial support to the unbanked and underbanked.

However, stringent KYC requirements may present barriers to entry for these populations, limiting their access to cryptocurrency services. Striking a balance between preventing illicit activities and ensuring financial inclusion is essential for leveraging the transformative potential of cryptocurrencies in underserved communities.

Advancements in technology are driving innovations in compliance and KYC processes. Blockchain-based identity solutions, decentralized identifiers (DIDs), and self-sovereign identity (SSI) frameworks are being explored as alternatives to traditional KYC practices.

These innovations aim to give individuals more control over their personal data, allowing them to share specific attributes with service providers without disclosing unnecessary information. Such solutions may address privacy concerns while maintaining compliance with regulatory requirements.

The global nature of cryptocurrencies calls for international collaboration and the development of common standards for compliance and KYC procedures. Global organizations, like the Financial Action Task Force (FATF), have taken steps to develop guidelines for cryptocurrency regulations to create a more cohesive and coordinated regulatory landscape.

Collaborative efforts among countries can help address regulatory challenges posed by cross-border cryptocurrency transactions, promoting a more secure and transparent global financial system.

In conclusion, compliance and KYC measures are crucial components of the cryptocurrency ecosystem, contributing to the prevention of money laundering, terrorist financing, and fraud and protecting user interests. While these measures come with challenges, including privacy concerns and potential barriers to financial inclusion, innovations in compliance technology and global collaboration offer opportunities to address these issues.

CHAPTER X

Understanding Initial Coin Offerings (ICOs)

What are ICOs?

Cryptocurrencies have transformed the landscape of fundraising, introducing a novel method known as Initial Coin Offerings (ICOs). Initial Coin Offerings (ICOs) have altered the way startups and blockchain projects raise funds by offering an alternative to conventional fundraising techniques like IPOs and venture capital. Startups and blockchain initiatives can generate funds by issuing new cryptocurrency tokens or coins through an initial coin offering (ICO). In an ICO, contributors and investors are given the chance to buy these tokens in return for fiat money like US dollars or existing cryptocurrencies like Bitcoin or Ethereum. The funds raised from the ICO are typically used to finance the development of the project and the underlying technology.

ICOs differ from traditional IPOs in that they do not involve the sale of shares in a company. Instead, investors receive newly created tokens, which may have various utilities within the project's ecosystem. Depending on the specific project, these tokens may represent digital assets, access rights, voting power, or other functionalities.

The process of conducting an ICO typically involves several key steps. First, the project team prepares a detailed whitepaper that outlines the project's objectives, the underlying technology, the use of funds raised, and the specific utility and functionality of the tokens. The whitepaper is an informational document for potential investors, providing insights into the project's potential and viability.

Next, the project team creates the new tokens on a blockchain platform, often using smart contracts. Smart contracts are self-executing agreements with the terms of the ICO embedded in the code. They facilitate the issuance, distribution, and management of the tokens, automating various aspects of the ICO process.

Some projects conduct a pre-sale or private sale phase before the main crowdsale. Early contributors and institutional investors can purchase tokens at discounted prices or with additional benefits during the pre-sale. The main crowdsale is open to the public, allowing anyone to participate and contribute funds to the project in exchange for tokens.

After the crowdsale, the project team distributes the purchased tokens to the investors' cryptocurrency wallets. Depending on the project, the tokens may become immediately tradable on cryptocurrency exchanges or subject to a lock-up period to prevent immediate sell-offs.

ICOs offer several advantages for both projects and investors. First, they provide access to capital for blockchain projects and startups, offering a streamlined and accessible method to raise funds from a global pool of investors. This democratization of fundraising allows projects with innovative ideas to secure funding without relying solely on traditional venture capital.

ICOs also have a global reach, enabling projects to attract investors worldwide. This accessibility breaks down geographical barriers and facilitates investment from individuals who may not have had the opportunity to participate in traditional fundraising methods.

Furthermore, ICOs create a community of early adopters and contributors who are incentivized to support the project's success. These early token holders often become advocates for the project, promoting its growth and adoption.

ICOs tokens can have various utilities and functionalities within the project's ecosystem. Investors may gain access to unique services, products, or voting rights, creating a sense of ownership and engagement with the project.

Despite these advantages, ICOs also come with certain risks and challenges. The lack of comprehensive regulation in the ICO space has led to instances of fraudulent projects and scams. Investors may become victims of fraudulent initial coin offerings (ICOs) that make unrealistic returns or break their promises.

The cryptocurrency market is also known for its high volatility and speculative nature. After the ICO, the value of the tokens may fluctuate significantly, leading to potential losses for investors.

Furthermore, the absence of regulatory oversight in many jurisdictions may expose investors to inadequate protection. Unlike traditional financial markets, ICO investments may not be insured or subject to investor safeguards.

Navigating the diverse regulatory landscape presents challenges for both ICO projects and investors. Compliance with multiple jurisdictions' regulatory requirements can be complex and costly, potentially limiting the accessibility of ICOs to a broader audience.

In conclusion, Initial Coin Offerings (ICOs) have emerged as a transformative fundraising method in the cryptocurrency and blockchain space. They offer advantages such as global accessibility, incentivized communities, and unique token functionalities. However, they also come with risks, including lack of regulation, market volatility, and investor protection concerns. To ensure the ongoing development and legitimacy of ICOs, it is essential to strike the proper balance between innovation and legal compliance. The role of ICOs will definitely change further as the cryptocurrency market develops, influencing how projects are funded and developed in the future digital era.

Evaluating ICOs: Potential and Risks

Cryptocurrencies and blockchain technology have witnessed a revolutionary fundraising method called Initial Coin Offerings

(ICOs). ICOs offer startups and blockchain projects an alternative means to raise capital, bypassing traditional financial institutions. However, the allure of ICOs and the promise of quick returns have also attracted unscrupulous actors, leading to concerns about fraudulent schemes and scams. In this section, we will explore the process of evaluating ICOs, their potential for both investors and projects, and the risks and challenges associated with participating in these crowdfunding campaigns.

An ICO is a fundraising event where investors and contributors offer a new cryptocurrency token or coin in exchange for established cryptocurrencies or fiat currencies. ICOs are typically conducted on blockchain platforms using smart contracts to facilitate the issuance and distribution of tokens.

To evaluate an ICO effectively, it is essential to understand its mechanics, including the project's goals, the technology it employs, the total supply of tokens, the distribution of tokens among team members and investors, and any vesting schedules. Additionally, investors should assess the whitepaper, which outlines the project's vision, use of funds, and the utility and functionality of the tokens.

ICOs offer several potential benefits to both projects and investors. First, they provide access to capital for blockchain projects, offering a direct avenue to raise funds from a global pool of investors. This democratization of fundraising allows projects with innovative ideas to secure funding without relying on traditional financial intermediaries.

ICOs also have a global reach, enabling projects to attract investors worldwide. Anyone with a computer or internet access can take part in the crowdfunding campaign as a result of this accessibility, which eliminates geographic restrictions.

Furthermore, ICOs foster a community of early adopters and contributors who are incentivized to support the project's success. These early token holders often become advocates for the project, helping to promote its growth and adoption.

ICO tokens may have various utilities and functionalities within the project's ecosystem. Investors may gain access to unique services, products, or voting rights, creating a sense of ownership and engagement with the project.

Investors should conduct thorough due diligence when evaluating ICO projects to assess their legitimacy and potential for success. Key factors to consider include the project team's credentials and expertise, the underlying technology and its potential real-world use case, the market demand for the project's product or service, the roadmap and milestones, and the project's community and communication channels.

Participating in ICOs also comes with significant risks and challenges. The lack of comprehensive regulation in the ICO space exposes investors to potential fraud and scams. Some projects may not adhere to best practices, leading to significant risks for investors.

Additionally, the value of ICO tokens may change significantly after the crowdsale due to the extreme volatility of the cryptocurrency market. Investors may experience significant gains or losses, depending on market sentiment.

Unlike traditional financial markets, ICO investments are often not subject to investor protection mechanisms. Investors may face challenges in seeking legal recourse in the event of a project's failure or misconduct.

Smart contract vulnerabilities and security breaches can lead to token theft and loss of funds. Investors should be cautious when participating in ICOs and ensure that they use secure wallets and follow best security practices.

The ICO space has become increasingly crowded, leading to market saturation and intense project competition. This saturation may make it challenging for some projects to stand out and gain investor attention.

Investors should adopt a cautious and thorough approach when evaluating ICOs to mitigate risks and make informed investment decisions. Conducting thorough due diligence, researching the project team, understanding the technology and use case, and assessing market demand are crucial steps in the evaluation process.

Staying informed about the regulatory landscape in different jurisdictions is also essential to comply with relevant laws and avoid potential legal pitfalls. Discussions between the project team and the community can yield insightful information on the state and potential of the project.

As the cryptocurrency and blockchain industry matures, regulatory frameworks, investor protection mechanisms, and more sustainable fundraising practices will likely emerge. By making informed decisions and exercising caution, investors can participate responsibly in ICOs and contribute to the growth and development of the cryptocurrency ecosystem. Ultimately, the success of ICOs relies on striking the right balance between innovation, investor protection, and regulatory compliance in this dynamic and transformative domain.

Tips for Participating in ICOs

Initial Coin Offerings (ICOs) have revolutionized how startups and blockchain projects raise capital, offering a direct and accessible method for investors to participate in crowdfunding campaigns. However, the rapid proliferation of ICOs has also increased the risk of scams and fraudulent schemes. As investors navigate this crowded and dynamic landscape, adopting a cautious and informed approach is crucial.

One of the most critical tips for participating in ICOs is to conduct thorough due diligence on the project and its team. Scrutinize the whitepaper to understand the project's objectives, technology, and use of funds. Evaluate the credentials and experience of the project team, assessing their past contributions to the blockchain and cryptocurrency space. A strong team with relevant expertise increases the project's credibility and potential for success.

Understanding the project's technology and use case is vital when evaluating ICOs. Assess the uniqueness and practicality of the project's solution and its potential to address real-world challenges. Projects with innovative and applicable use cases are more likely to gain traction and deliver long-term value.

Evaluate the market demand for the project's product or service. A strong market demand indicates the potential for adoption and growth. Research the existing competition and consider how the project differentiates itself in the market. Assess whether the project offers unique features, partnerships, or advantages that set it apart from competitors.

Examine the project's roadmap and the milestones it aims to achieve. A clear and achievable roadmap demonstrates the project's commitment to a well-defined development path. Consider the timeline for delivering key milestones and whether the project team has a realistic approach to reaching their goals.

Beware of ICO projects that make unrealistic claims or promises of high returns with little or no risk. Investing in ICOs involves risks; no investment is guaranteed to yield profits. Exercise caution if the project emphasizes the potential for massive returns without adequately explaining the underlying value proposition and market potential.

Understand the utility and functionality of the tokens being offered in the ICO. Determine whether the tokens have a clear purpose within the project's ecosystem. Tokens that provide real utility, such as access to products or services, governance rights, or rewards, will likely have long-term value.

Diversification is a fundamental principle of investing. Avoid putting all your funds into a single ICO project. Instead, consider spreading your investments across multiple projects with promising fundamentals. Diversification helps mitigate the impact of potential losses from individual investments.

Different ICOs employ various fundraising structures, such as a fixed price per token, tiered pricing, or dynamic pricing based on demand. Each structure has its advantages and risks. Evaluate the fairness and transparency of the pricing mechanism to ensure that all participants have an equal opportunity to invest.

The regulatory landscape surrounding ICOs is continuously evolving. Stay informed about the legal and regulatory requirements in your jurisdiction. Compliance with relevant regulations is essential to protect your investments and avoid legal issues.

When taking part in ICOs, the security of your money is significant. As you store your tokens, use safe wallets and adhere to recommended security practices, such turning on two-factor authentication and keeping your private keys offline.

Be prepared for price fluctuations in the value of ICO tokens after the crowdsale. The cryptocurrency market is known for its high volatility. Refrain from making investment choices on emotions based on quick price changes.

Avoid the fear of missing out (FOMO), which can lead to impulsive investment decisions. Take the time to evaluate each ICO project thoroughly and don't succumb to pressure or hype. Making well-informed decisions based on research and analysis is key to successful ICO investments.

Participating in ICOs can be a rewarding and exciting venture but comes with risks and challenges. By conducting thorough due diligence, understanding the project's technology and use case, and assessing market demand and competition, investors can make informed decisions and identify promising ICO projects.

Remember to stay informed about regulatory developments, diversify your investment portfolio, and use secure wallets to protect your funds. Exercise caution when evaluating ICO projects and avoid falling for unrealistic promises or FOMO-driven investment decisions.

By following these essential tips, investors can navigate the crowded crowdfunding landscape and contribute to the growth and development of the cryptocurrency and blockchain ecosystem while safeguarding their investments and financial well-being.

CHAPTER XI

Cryptocurrency Security and Risks

Common Security Threats

Cryptocurrencies have gained widespread popularity as digital assets that promise decentralized and secure transactions. However, the rapidly evolving landscape of cryptocurrencies also brings forth various security threats that investors and users must be aware of. The interest of malicious individuals looking to take advantage of vulnerabilities in the system increases as the value and use of cryptocurrency rises. This section will explore the most common security threats in the cryptocurrency space, their potential risks, and essential measures to safeguard digital assets.

Phishing attacks are one of the most prevalent security threats in cryptocurrency. In a phishing attack, scammers use deceptive emails, websites, or messages to trick users into disclosing sensitive information, like the login credentials or private keys. Unsuspecting users may inadvertently provide access to their cryptocurrency wallets, leading to the theft of their digital assets.

To protect against phishing attacks, users should exercise caution when clicking links or providing personal information. Always verify the authenticity of the website or communication before entering sensitive data. Using hardware wallets or cold storage solutions can also provide an added layer of protection against phishing attempts.

Malware and keyloggers are malicious software that can compromise the security of cryptocurrency wallets and exchanges. Keyloggers record keystrokes and can capture sensitive information, including passwords and private keys. Malware can infect computers and smartphones, providing unauthorized access to digital assets.

To mitigate this threat, users should regularly update their antivirus software and avoid downloading files or applications from untrusted sources. Enabling two-factor authentication (2FA) adds an extra security layer to protect against unauthorized access.

Cryptocurrency exchanges are platforms for buying, selling, and trading digital assets. However, they are also prime targets for hackers due to the large sums of cryptocurrencies stored in their wallets. Exchange hacks and security breaches have resulted in significant losses for users and exchanges.

Users should choose reputable and well-established exchanges with a strong security track record to reduce the risk of falling victim to exchange hacks. Storing a significant portion of funds in personal wallets rather than on exchanges can also limit potential losses in case of a security breach.

The anonymous nature of cryptocurrencies has facilitated the rise of Ponzi schemes and investment scams. In these schemes, fraudsters promise high returns on investments but ultimately use funds from new investors to pay returns to earlier investors. Eventually, the scheme collapses, leaving most participants with losses.

Investors should exercise skepticism and conduct thorough due diligence on any investment opportunity to avoid falling for Ponzi schemes and scams. Avoiding investments that promise unrealistic returns or lack transparency is crucial in safeguarding against such scams.

Social engineering attacks exploit human psychology to manipulate users into revealing sensitive information or making unauthorized transactions. Attackers may use social media, phone calls, or other communication channels to deceive individuals into divulging private information.

To protect against social engineering attacks, users should be cautious about sharing personal information and avoid responding to unsolicited requests for sensitive data. Verifying the identity of the person or organization before sharing any information is essential in thwarting social engineering attempts.

Malicious actors may create fake mobile apps that mimic legitimate cryptocurrency wallets or exchanges. Users downloading and using these fake apps unknowingly expose their private keys or login credentials to attackers.

To avoid falling for fake mobile apps, users should only download applications from official app stores and verify the app's authenticity before entering sensitive data. Checking app reviews and developer information can help identify potential fraudulent apps.

Pump-and-dump schemes entail artificially inflating the price of a cryptocurrency through misleading or false information, only to sell it at a higher price once unsuspecting investors have bought in. These schemes can lead to significant losses for investors who buy in during the pump phase.

To protect against pump-and-dump schemes, investors should thoroughly research the projects they are interested in and be cautious about acting on information from unknown sources or unverified claims.

Insider threats occur when individuals with access to sensitive information abuse their privileges to exploit vulnerabilities in the system. In cryptocurrencies, this could involve employees or contractors with access to private keys or sensitive data using it for unauthorized purposes.

Organizations and cryptocurrency service providers should develop strong security measures, run personnel background checks, and restrict access to sensitive information to those who need it in order to reduce insider risks.

In conclusion, cryptocurrencies offer exciting opportunities for investors and users. However, it also presents various security threats that require vigilance and caution. Phishing attacks, malware, exchange hacks, and Ponzi schemes are some of the common security threats that users must be aware of and take measures to protect against.

Best Practices for Securing Your Investments

Cryptocurrencies have emerged as a groundbreaking financial asset class, promising decentralization, security, and potential for substantial returns. However, the decentralized nature of cryptocurrencies also exposes users to unique security risks. As the adoption of digital assets grows, it becomes essential for investors and users to prioritize security and adopt best practices to safeguard their investments.

One of the most crucial best practices for securing cryptocurrency investments is to use hardware wallets. Hardware wallets are tangible objects made to safely store private keys in offline locations. Hardware wallets significantly reduce the risk of online attacks and theft by keeping private keys offline, away from internet-connected devices. Hardware wallets provide an added layer of protection against malware, phishing attempts, and other digital threats.

Enabling two-factor authentication (2FA) is another essential security measure for cryptocurrency accounts and wallets. By requiring a second form of verification in addition to the password, which could be a unique code sent to a mobile device, 2FA offers a further layer of protection. This prevents unauthorized access even if an attacker has obtained the login credentials.

When trading or investing in cryptocurrencies, it is crucial to use reputable and secure exchanges. Conduct thorough research to select exchanges with a strong security and customer support track record. Look for exchanges implementing robust security measures, such as cold storage for funds and regular security audits.

Securing private keys is of utmost importance in protecting cryptocurrency holdings. Private keys are the cryptographic keys that grant access to digital assets. Always keep your private keys secure and avoid sharing them with anyone. Ideally, store private keys offline or use hardware wallets to ensure they are not vulnerable to online attacks.

Regularly updating software and devices is essential to stay protected against the latest security threats. Users should keep their operating systems, antivirus software, and cryptocurrency wallet applications current. Security patches and bug fixes that guard against known vulnerabilities are frequently included in updates.

Hackers frequently utilize phishing attacks to get sensitive data, such as login credentials or private keys. Exercise caution while opening attachments or accessing links from unidentified sources. Always verify the authenticity of websites and communication before providing any personal information.

Implementing secure password practices is vital to protecting cryptocurrency holdings. Strong and unique passwords should be used to prevent unauthorized access. Avoid employing passwords that are quick to guess or utilizing the same password across many accounts. To create and securely store complicated passwords, think about utilizing a reliable password manager.

A crucial risk-management strategy in investing is diversification. Do not invest all of the funds you have in one cryptocurrency. Spreading your investments across multiple digital assets can help mitigate the impact of price fluctuations or security breaches affecting a particular cryptocurrency.

Monitoring cryptocurrency exchange accounts and wallet balances is essential to detect and promptly respond to suspicious activity. Users should report any unauthorized transactions or security concerns to the exchange or wallet provider and take appropriate actions to secure their funds.

Educating yourself about the latest security risks and best practices in the cryptocurrency industry is crucial. Engaging in online communities and forums can provide valuable insights from experienced users and security experts. The more you know about security risks, the better equipped you'll be to protect your investments.

Consider using multi-signature wallets for added security. Multi-signature wallets need multiple private keys to authorize transactions, making it more challenging for attackers to gain unauthorized access.

Keep personal information private and avoid sharing sensitive information with anyone, such as private keys or wallet recovery phrases. Be cautious about sharing cryptocurrency investment details publicly, as it can make you a target for malicious actors.

Backing up cryptocurrency wallets and keeping the backup files safe and secure is essential. In the event of a hardware failure or loss of access, having a backup ensures that you can recover your funds and regain access to your accounts.

Avoid storing significant amounts of cryptocurrency on exchanges for extended periods. While exchanges provide liquidity and convenience for trading, they are also more vulnerable to security breaches. Move funds to secure offline storage or hardware wallets when not actively trading.

Staying cautious of third-party services that require access to your cryptocurrency wallets or private keys is crucial. Always verify the reputation and security measures of such services before using them.

In conclusion, securing cryptocurrency investments is a paramount responsibility for users in the digital assets' dynamic and evolving landscape. By adopting best practices, such as utilizing hardware wallets, enabling two-factor authentication, choosing reputable exchanges, and regularly updating software, investors can significantly enhance the security of their cryptocurrency holdings. Staying informed about the most recent security risks and industry developments is essential in safeguarding investments and maintaining financial well-being. Embracing a security-conscious mindset is fundamental in maximizing the benefits of cryptocurrency investments while minimizing exposure to potential risks.

Scams and Ponzi Schemes to Avoid

The cryptocurrency world offers exciting opportunities for investors seeking to participate in the digital asset revolution. However, this dynamic and decentralized landscape also attracts malicious actors and scammers looking to exploit the growing interest in cryptocurrencies. Scams and Ponzi schemes have become prevalent in cryptocurrency, posing significant risks to investors' hard-earned funds.

One of the most common types of scams in the cryptocurrency realm is the Initial Coin Offering (ICO) scam. ICOs are crowdfunding events where cryptocurrency projects raise funds by selling tokens to investors. While many legitimate projects have successfully utilized ICOs to fund their developments, ICO scams are unfortunate. Scammers may publish a compelling whitepaper with unrealistic promises to lure investors. Sometimes, they may even create fake teams or use false credentials to appear credible. Once they have raised funds from unsuspecting investors, scammers vanish without delivering on their promises, leaving investors with worthless tokens. Investors should conduct thorough due diligence on projects before investing to avoid ICO scams. Scrutinize the project's whitepaper, team credentials, and technology. Look for projects with active and transparent communities and those that provide regular updates on their progress.

Ponzi schemes are among the oldest and most notorious types of scams and have found their way into the cryptocurrency space. In a typical Ponzi scheme, early investors are paid returns using funds from newer investors, creating the illusion of a profitable venture.

However, as more people join the scheme, it becomes unsustainable, and most participants eventually lose their investments. In cryptocurrency, Ponzi schemes may masquerade as investment clubs or programs offering guaranteed high returns. They often promise to use investors' funds for trading or other activities, but instead, they rely on new investments to pay returns to existing participants. To avoid falling victim to Ponzi schemes, be cautious of investment opportunities that guarantee high returns with little or no risk. Conduct extensive research on any investment program, and avoid participating in ventures that lack transparency or proof of actual activities.

Another common scam in the cryptocurrency space involves fake airdrops and giveaways. Airdrops and giveaways are marketing strategies legitimate cryptocurrency projects use to distribute tokens to their community members or attract new users. However, scammers have capitalized on this practice to deceive individuals into providing their private keys or personal information. Fake airdrops and giveaways are usually promoted on social media platforms or messaging apps. Scammers may impersonate well-known projects or influencers, offering free tokens in exchange for personal data. Once users provide their private keys or sensitive information, scammers can access their cryptocurrency wallets and steal their funds. To avoid fake airdrop scams, always verify the authenticity of any promotion before participating. Official announcements are typically made on the project's official website or social media channels. Never share your private keys or sensitive information with unknown individuals or entities.

Pump-and-dump schemes are a kind of market manipulation in which coordinated groups artificially inflate the price of a low-value cryptocurrency, only to sell their holdings at the peak, causing the price to collapse. Unsuspecting investors who buy in during the pump phase experience significant losses when the price plummets. Pump-and-dump schemes often spread through social media groups and online forums. Scammers use false or exaggerated claims to attract investors to the targeted cryptocurrency. Once the price reaches a certain level, the group behind the scheme sells their holdings, causing panic selling among other investors. To protect against pump-and-dump schemes, avoid acting on information from unknown sources or unverified claims. Conduct thorough research on any cryptocurrency before making investment decisions, and avoid FOMO-driven (Fear of Missing Out) purchases during price spikes.

Malware and phishing scams are also common tactics used by hackers to steal cryptocurrency from unsuspecting users. Malware can infect computers and smartphones, granting attackers access to cryptocurrency wallets and private keys. Phishing scams involve fraudulent emails, websites, or messages made to trick users into disclosing sensitive information. To protect against malware and phishing scams, users should employ robust antivirus software, regularly update their devices and software, and avoid downloading files from untrusted sources. Always verify websites and communications' authenticity before providing personal or sensitive data.

Fake or impersonated exchanges are another threat in the cryptocurrency space. Scammers may create fake cryptocurrency exchange websites that closely mimic the design and layout of legitimate exchanges. Unsuspecting users may unknowingly sign up on these fake platforms, providing their login credentials and depositing funds, only to realize later that they have fallen victim to a scam. To avoid fake exchange scams, use reputable and well-established exchanges with a strong track record of security and customer support. Double-check the website URL and domain to ensure you are on the official exchange platform. To avoid visiting fake exchange websites, don't click on links in unsolicited messages or emails.

The number of frauds and Ponzi schemes that prey on unwary investors is growing along with the popularity of cryptocurrencies. Individuals need to be on the lookout for scams of all types and be aware of them in order to protect their investments. Avoid falling for ICO scams, Ponzi schemes, and fake airdrops by conducting thorough due diligence and verifying the authenticity of investment opportunities. Protect against pump-and-dump schemes, malware, and phishing scams by staying cautious of unknown sources and regularly updating security measures. By adopting a careful approach and adhering to best practices, investors can confidently navigate the cryptocurrency landscape, reducing their exposure to scams and Ponzi schemes, and maximizing the potential benefits of this revolutionary financial asset class.

CHAPTER XII

Cryptocurrency and the Future

The Impact of Cryptocurrencies on Traditional Finance

Cryptocurrencies have revolutionized the financial landscape, challenging traditional financial systems and transforming how we perceive and interact with money. Cryptocurrencies, with their decentralized nature and underlying blockchain technology, have gained popularity as an alternative to traditional fiat currencies and financial intermediaries. In this section, we will explore the impact of cryptocurrencies on traditional finance, analyzing their potential benefits and drawbacks in reshaping the global financial ecosystem.

One of the significant impacts of cryptocurrencies on traditional finance is the potential to promote financial inclusion and accessibility. In many parts of the world, conventional banking services are unavailable or inaccessible to a significant portion of the population. Cryptocurrencies, being digital and decentralized, offer an opportunity for the unbanked and underbanked to participate in the global financial system. With just a digital wallet and an internet connection, individuals can send and receive cryptocurrencies, enabling them to engage in financial transactions without needing a traditional bank account.

Cryptocurrencies challenge conventional financial intermediaries by operating on decentralized blockchain networks. The absence of central authorities or intermediaries, such as banks or payment processors, means that transactions can be conducted directly between peers. This disintermediation can potentially reduce transaction costs and increase efficiency in the financial system. Additionally, it empowers individuals to have greater control over their financial assets and transactions.

Traditional cross-border transactions and remittances can be time-consuming and costly, involving multiple intermediaries and currency conversions. Cryptocurrencies facilitate borderless transactions, enabling faster and more cost-effective cross-border transfers. This has significant implications for global trade, investment, and remittance flows, especially for individuals in countries with limited access to traditional banking services.

The rise of cryptocurrencies has fueled financial innovation, leading to the development of various financial products and services. Tokenization, the process of representing real-world assets as digital tokens on blockchain networks, has gained traction. This development has the potential to completely alter asset ownership, investment, and trade by opening up a wider variety of investors to previously illiquid assets.

The impact of cryptocurrencies on traditional finance is not without challenges. Regulatory frameworks worldwide are struggling to keep pace with the rapid evolution of the cryptocurrency space. Cryptocurrencies' decentralized and borderless nature makes it difficult for individual countries to implement consistent and effective regulations. As a result, there is a lack of clarity on taxation, consumer protection, and anti-money laundering measures, leading to concerns about illicit activities and potential market manipulation.

Cryptocurrencies are known for their high price volatility, which poses risks for investors and traditional financial markets. The extreme price fluctuations observed in the cryptocurrency market can lead to significant gains but also substantial losses. The speculative nature of cryptocurrency investments has raised concerns about investor protection and the potential systemic risks to traditional financial institutions if a major cryptocurrency market correction occurs.

As cryptocurrencies gain popularity, several central banks have explored the concept of Central Bank Digital Currencies (CBDCs). A CBDC is a digital form of a country's fiat currency issued and regulated by its central bank. CBDCs aim to combine the advantages of digital currencies with the stability and backing of traditional fiat currencies. The development and implementation of CBDCs may be able to close the gap between cryptocurrencies and traditional finance while providing the benefits of both.

The growing adoption of cryptocurrencies as a payment method is challenging traditional payment systems and financial infrastructure.

Several merchants and businesses now accept cryptocurrencies as a valid form of payment, and some financial institutions have begun to integrate cryptocurrency services into their offerings. This changing landscape is prompting traditional financial institutions to adapt and explore innovative solutions to meet the demands of the evolving market.

Cryptocurrencies offer a degree of financial privacy, as transactions are pseudonymous and not directly linked to personal information. While this may be advantageous for privacy-conscious users, it has also raised concerns about the potential misuse of cryptocurrencies for illicit activities, such as money laundering and terrorism financing. Regulators and policymakers are grappling with striking the right balance between privacy and ensuring the financial system's integrity.

The increasing popularity of cryptocurrencies has sparked debates about their impact on traditional monetary policy and economic stability. Central banks may face challenges in conducting monetary policy when cryptocurrencies become more widely adopted. Additionally, the potential shift of funds from traditional banking systems to cryptocurrencies could affect conventional lending practices and economic stability.

In conclusion, the impact of cryptocurrencies on traditional finance is multifaceted, with both potential benefits and challenges. Cryptocurrencies have the ability to promote financial inclusion, revolutionize cross-border transactions, and foster financial innovation. However, the lack of regulatory clarity, price volatility, and concerns about investor protection highlight the need for a balanced and comprehensive approach to harnessing the potential benefits while addressing the challenges.

As the cryptocurrency space continues to evolve, it will be essential for regulators, policymakers, and financial institutions to collaborate in developing a robust regulatory framework that fosters innovation while safeguarding financial stability and consumer protection. Striking the right balance between decentralization and regulation will be crucial in utilizing the full potential of cryptocurrencies to transform and enhance the global financial ecosystem. As traditional finance and cryptocurrencies continue to interact and evolve, market participants must remain informed and adaptive to the changing landscape, ensuring a secure and prosperous financial future for all.

The Role of Central Banks and Governments

The rapid rise of cryptocurrencies has raised significant questions about the role of central banks and governments in this emerging financial landscape. Cryptocurrencies, with their decentralized nature and borderless transactions, challenge the traditional monetary and regulatory frameworks that central banks and governments have long maintained. In this section, we will explore the role of central banks and governments in cryptocurrency and its potential implications for the future of finance.

Central banks play a crucial role in issuing and regulating fiat currencies, the traditional currencies nations use. The occurence of cryptocurrencies has prompted central banks to evaluate their stance on these digital assets. Some central banks are exploring the idea of

Central Bank Digital Currencies (CBDCs), which are digital versions of their respective fiat currencies issued and regulated by the central bank. The development of CBDCs aims to combine the advantages of digital currencies, such as fast and cost-effective transactions, with the stability and backing of traditional fiat currencies. CBDCs can potentially enhance the efficiency of payments, reduce transaction costs, and enable better monetary policy implementation.

Cryptocurrencies' decentralized and cross-border nature presents unique regulatory challenges for governments and central banks. Cryptocurrencies operate on blockchain networks, which are distributed ledgers that store transaction records across a vast network of computers. This decentralized nature makes it difficult for any single entity, including central banks or governments, to control the cryptocurrency market completely. Regulatory frameworks are evolving to address concerns related to consumer protection, money laundering, tax evasion, and financial stability in the context of cryptocurrencies.

The growing popularity of cryptocurrencies has raised concerns about potential systemic risks to the financial system. Cryptocurrencies' high volatility and speculative nature can lead to significant price fluctuations, impacting investor confidence and traditional financial markets. Moreover, integrating cryptocurrencies with the conventional financial system may expose banks and financial institutions to new risks. These trends are being actively watched by central banks, which are also evaluating any possible threats to financial stability.

Cryptocurrencies' decentralization challenges the traditional mechanisms through which central banks conduct monetary policy. With cryptocurrencies being beyond the direct control of any central authority, traditional tools such as interest rate adjustments may have limited impact on cryptocurrency markets. Additionally, the shift of funds from traditional banking systems to cryptocurrencies could affect money supply, inflation, and other macroeconomic indicators. Central banks are exploring ways to adapt their monetary policy frameworks to account for the influence of cryptocurrencies on the broader economy.

The decentralized nature of cryptocurrencies also means that consumers may have limited recourse in cases of fraud, hacking, or loss of funds. Unlike traditional banking systems, cryptocurrency transactions are generally irreversible, making it essential for consumers to exercise caution and take responsibility for securing their assets. Governments and central banks are working hard to inform the public about the advantages and disadvantages of cryptocurrencies as well as the value of using secure management techniques for digital assets.

The role of central banks and governments in cryptocurrency is a balancing act between fostering innovation and ensuring financial stability and consumer protection. While embracing the potential benefits of cryptocurrencies and blockchain technology, regulators must also address potential risks to the financial system and economy. Striking the right balance will require collaboration between governments, central banks, financial institutions, and the cryptocurrency industry.

The global nature of cryptocurrencies calls for international cooperation and standardization in regulating these assets. As cryptocurrencies do not recognize national borders, a unified approach to regulatory frameworks can help address potential regulatory arbitrage and create a level playing field for market participants. International organizations like the Financial Stability Board and the International Monetary Fund are trying to promote communication and collaboration among nations on issues relating to cryptocurrencies.

Governments and central banks continuously adapt their policies and frameworks to keep pace with the rapidly evolving cryptocurrency landscape. Many countries have introduced or proposed specific regulations for cryptocurrency exchanges, initial coin offerings (ICOs), and anti-money laundering measures. However, there is still a need for greater regulatory clarity and harmonization to promote innovation and provide a stable regulatory environment for businesses and investors.

Cryptocurrencies and blockchain technology have spurred innovation in the financial industry. Governments and central banks are increasingly exploring the potential use cases of blockchain beyond cryptocurrencies, such as in digital identity, supply chain management, and healthcare. Collaborative efforts between the public and private sectors can foster responsible innovation and unlock the full potential of blockchain technology to benefit various sectors of the economy.

The role of central banks and governments in cryptocurrency will continue to evolve as these digital assets become more integrated into the global financial system. CBDCs will likely play a significant role in the future, providing governments with additional tools for monetary policy and financial inclusion. The regulation of cryptocurrencies will become increasingly crucial as adoption and investment grow. Governments must balance fostering innovation and ensuring financial stability, consumer protection, and compliance with international standards.

Predictions for the Future of Cryptocurrencies

Since the appearance of Bitcoin in 2009, the world of cryptocurrencies has experienced fast growth and evolution. Over the past decade, these digital assets have gained widespread attention and adoption, disrupting traditional financial systems and sparking debates about their future trajectory. In this section, we will explore various predictions for the future of cryptocurrencies, considering both optimistic and cautious viewpoints. While the future remains uncertain, examining potential scenarios can help us better understand the possible paths cryptocurrencies may take in the years ahead.

One of the most widely held predictions for cryptocurrencies is their increased mainstream adoption and integration into various industries. As more individuals and businesses become familiar with cryptocurrencies, we can expect to see greater acceptance as a means of payment and investment. Cryptocurrencies could become a standard part of everyday financial transactions, complementing or even competing with traditional fiat currencies. Further innovation and use cases might be sparked by combining cryptocurrencies with innovative technologies like the Internet of Things (IoT) and smart contracts.

In reaction to the rise of cryptocurrencies, central banks all over the world are looking into the concept of CBDCs or Central Bank Digital Currencies. CBDCs are electronic equivalents of a nation's fiat currency that are created and governed by the central bank. Several countries are already piloting or researching CBDCs, and their development could be a game-changer for cryptocurrency. While CBDCs aim to combine the benefits of digital currencies with the stability of fiat, their success could also influence the future adoption and regulation of existing cryptocurrencies.

Privacy concerns have been a prominent topic in the cryptocurrency space. As cryptocurrencies evolve, we expect to see improved privacy features and protocols. Technologies like Zero-Knowledge Proofs and Secure Multi-Party Computation are being explored to enhance transaction privacy. Additionally, advancements in secure wallet technologies and multi-factor authentication may reduce the risk of cyberattacks and improve the overall security of cryptocurrency storage.

Institutional investors are already beginning to enter the cryptocurrency sector. We see a spike in institutional investment in cryptocurrencies as the market develops and regulatory clarity increases. This influx of capital may lead to the development of more sophisticated financial products, such as cryptocurrency-based exchange-traded funds (ETFs), derivatives, and structured products. These developments could bring more liquidity and stability to the cryptocurrency market.

The proliferation of various blockchain networks and cryptocurrencies has raised challenges in terms of interoperability and seamless exchange between different assets. The future may witness the development of cross-chain solutions and protocols, allowing for efficient transfer of value and data across different blockchain networks. This interoperability could foster greater collaboration and efficiency in the decentralized finance (DeFi) space.

The rise of DeFi has been one of the most significant trends in the cryptocurrency space. DeFi platforms enable various financial services, such as lending, borrowing, and yield farming, without traditional intermediaries. As the DeFi ecosystem grows, we can expect to see more tokenization of assets, where real-world assets are represented as digital tokens on blockchain networks. This could democratize access to traditional financial instruments and create new investment opportunities.

Cryptocurrencies have faced regulatory uncertainty in various jurisdictions. As the industry matures, governments worldwide may work together to establish clearer and consistent regulatory frameworks for cryptocurrencies. International cooperation may lead to more cohesive policies that promote innovation while addressing consumer protection, anti-money laundering, and market integrity concerns.

The environmental impact of cryptocurrency mining has drawn scrutiny due to the energy-intensive process required for proof-of-work consensus algorithms. In the future, we expect to see more sustainable and energy-efficient consensus mechanisms, such as proof-of-stake and hybrid models. Additionally, advancements in renewable energy sources could alleviate environmental concerns associated with cryptocurrency mining.

The cryptocurrency space is highly competitive, and numerous projects are vying for market dominance. In the future, technological advancements and innovative use cases will continue to emerge, leading to healthy competition and market evolution. Projects that can demonstrate practical utility and scalability will probably have an advantage in the market.

While many predictions are optimistic, it is essential to acknowledge the uncertainties and challenges that cryptocurrencies face. Regulatory environments may evolve unpredictably, affecting the growth and adoption of cryptocurrencies. Additionally, technological hurdles, security threats, and potential market manipulations may threaten the stability and credibility of the entire cryptocurrency ecosystem.

CONCLUSION

Embracing the Cryptocurrency Revolution

The emergence of cryptocurrencies has sparked a revolution in the world of finance and technology. Bitcoin, the pioneer cryptocurrency, introduced the concept of decentralized digital assets, challenging the traditional financial system's centralization and intermediation. Since then, thousands of other cryptocurrencies have been developed, each with distinct features and applications. With the launch of Bitcoin in 2009, an unidentified person or group operating under the alias Satoshi Nakamoto kicked off the cryptocurrency revolution. Blockchain technology, a decentralized, open-source public ledger that keeps track of all financial transactions over a computer network, was popularized by Bitcoin. Blockchain's tamper-resistant nature and the ability to verify transactions without intermediaries laid the foundation for the cryptocurrency revolution.

One of the primary drivers of the cryptocurrency revolution is its potential to disrupt traditional finance. With the use of cryptocurrencies, consumers can send and receive money anywhere in the world without the need for banks or other financial organizations to facilitate the transaction. Financial inclusion may increase as a result of this development, particularly in areas with limited access to conventional banking services.

Cryptocurrencies have democratized investment opportunities by providing access to innovative projects and assets to a broader audience. Initial Coin Offerings (ICOs) and token sales allow startups and projects to raise funds directly from the public, reducing the reliance on venture capital and traditional funding sources. This democratization has empowered retail investors to participate in early-stage investment opportunities previously limited to accredited investors.

Beyond digital currencies, the cryptocurrency revolution has fostered the development of decentralized applications (DApps). These are applications built on blockchain networks that operate without a central authority. DApps offer various services, including decentralized finance (DeFi), gaming, supply chain management, and more. The flexibility and transparency of blockchain have opened new possibilities for DApp developers and users alike.

The cryptocurrency revolution has not been without challenges. Regulatory uncertainty remains a significant hurdle in the widespread adoption of cryptocurrencies. Governments worldwide grapple with how to regulate and tax these digital assets, which sometimes fall into gray areas of existing financial regulations. It is a difficult endeavor that calls for careful analysis and cooperation between regulators and the cryptocurrency industry to strike the correct balance between innovation and consumer safety.

The cryptocurrency market is notorious for its price volatility. While this volatility presents investment opportunities, it also poses risks for investors and businesses. The value of cryptocurrencies can experience substantial swings in short periods, leading to potential financial losses for traders and investors. Managing risk and adopting a long-term investment strategy are essential for those venturing into the cryptocurrency market.

Security is critical to cryptocurrencies, as they rely on cryptographic keys for access and ownership. The responsibility of securing private keys lies with the users themselves. Private key theft or loss might result in a permanent loss of funds. Additionally, the reliance on cryptocurrency exchanges and custodial services introduces counterparty risks, as some exchanges have been subject to hacking incidents.

The energy-intensive process of cryptocurrency mining has raised concerns about its environmental impact, particularly for proof-of-work consensus algorithms. Critics argue that mining contributes to carbon emissions and exacerbates energy consumption. In response, some cryptocurrencies are exploring energy-efficient consensus mechanisms like proof-of-stake to address these environmental concerns.

By giving the unbanked and underbanked populations access to financial services, the revolution in cryptocurrency has the potential to advance financial inclusion. With a smartphone and internet connection, individuals can participate in the cryptocurrency ecosystem and access services such as savings, loans, and remittances without needing a traditional bank account.

Cryptocurrencies offer an alternative for cross-border transactions, bypassing the need for traditional banking intermediaries and expensive international wire transfers. This efficiency and cost-effectiveness have the potential to reshape the global remittance market, benefiting individuals and businesses that rely on cross-border transactions.

In conclusion, the cryptocurrency revolution has ushered in a new era of finance and technology, disrupting traditional financial systems and empowering individuals with financial autonomy. While it presents numerous opportunities for financial inclusion, investment, and technological advancement, the cryptocurrency space also faces regulation, security, and sustainability challenges. Embracing the cryptocurrency revolution requires a balanced approach that harnesses its potential while addressing risks and uncertainties. As the industry continues to evolve, collaboration between governments, businesses, and individuals will be vital to unlocking the full potential of cryptocurrencies in shaping the future of finance and technology.

Final Thoughts and Takeaways

Throughout this comprehensive exploration of cryptocurrencies, blockchain technology, and their impact on various aspects of society, we have gained valuable insights into the revolutionary world of digital assets. The emergence of cryptocurrencies, with Bitcoin leading the way, marked the birth of a transformational technology that challenges traditional financial systems' centralization. Blockchain, the underlying innovation powering cryptocurrencies, has showcased its potential to revolutionize various industries through its transparency, security, and tamper-resistant nature.

One of the most significant achievements of the cryptocurrency revolution has been the democratization of finance. Initial Coin Offerings (ICOs) and token sales have opened up new opportunities for startups and projects to raise capital directly from the public, reducing the reliance on traditional funding sources. This democratization has enabled retail investors worldwide to participate in early-stage investment opportunities, leveling the playing field and fostering innovation.

The cryptocurrency revolution has its share of difficulties, though, as with any transformational technology. Regulatory uncertainty and varying approaches to cryptocurrency regulation worldwide have posed obstacles to broader adoption. Governments and regulatory bodies face the delicate task of balancing embracing innovation and protecting consumers and investors from potential risks. Unlocking the entire potential of cryptocurrencies and blockchain technologies will require achieving regulatory certainty and encouraging responsible innovation.

Beyond cryptocurrencies, blockchain technology has demonstrated its potential to revolutionize industries. Its decentralized and immutable nature promises to enhance efficiency, transparency, and security in supply chain management, healthcare, real estate, voting systems, and more. As technology evolves, its impact on these sectors will likely grow, shaping the future of various industries.

Addressing environmental concerns remains a priority for the cryptocurrency and blockchain ecosystem. The energy-intensive nature of cryptocurrency mining, particularly for proof-of-work consensus algorithms, has raised environmental concerns. While some cryptocurrencies are exploring more energy-efficient consensus mechanisms, balancing technological innovation with environmental responsibility will be crucial in the journey toward a more sustainable future.

The rise of decentralized finance (DeFi) has been one of the most significant trends in the cryptocurrency space. Without the use of middlemen, decentralized finance platforms provide a variety of financial services like lending, borrowing, as well as yield farming. Although DeFi has the potential to challenge conventional finance, it also poses risks and regulatory difficulties that must be carefully considered. Navigating this emerging landscape will require collaborative efforts from the industry and regulators.

Education and awareness are critical in fostering responsible adoption of cryptocurrencies and blockchain technology. Understanding the technology, risks, and potential benefits empowers individuals and businesses to make informed decisions. Public and private sectors alike should invest in educational initiatives to promote a well-informed and inclusive cryptocurrency ecosystem.

Investing in cryptocurrencies carries inherent risks due to their price volatility and regulatory uncertainties. Investors must approach the cryptocurrency market cautiously, conducting thorough research and understanding the potential risks. As with any investment, diversification and a long-term perspective are fundamental strategies for mitigating risk.

The future of cryptocurrencies and blockchain technology will depend on collaboration between various stakeholders, including governments, businesses, developers, and the public. Collaborative efforts will drive innovation and facilitate the creation of robust and scalable solutions that address real-world challenges. Moreover, open dialogue and cooperation between the public and private sectors will help foster an environment conducive to responsible and sustainable growth.

In conclusion, the cryptocurrency and blockchain technology journey has been enlightening and thought-provoking. From the birth of Bitcoin to the expansion of DeFi, we have witnessed the transformative power of digital assets. The cryptocurrency revolution represents a unique opportunity to reshape finance, technology, and society as a whole. As we move forward, striking the right balance between innovation, regulation, and environmental responsibility will be crucial in maximizing the benefits of this revolutionary technology. By embracing collaboration and seizing the opportunities presented, we can collectively shape a more inclusive, efficient, and sustainable future powered by cryptocurrencies and blockchain.

Thank you for buying and reading/listening to our book. If you found this book useful/helpful please take a few minutes and leave a review on the platform where you purchased our book. Your feedback matters greatly to us.